JUDGMENT UNTO TRUTH

1. *Rev. Ephraim Jernazian.*
(Jernazian family collection.)

JUDGMENT UNTO TRUTH
Witnessing the Armenian Genocide

Ephraim K. Jernazian
Translated by
Alice Haig

Transaction Publishers
New Brunswick (U.S.A.) and London (U.K.)

Library of Congress Catalog Number: 89-20662
ISBN: 0-888738-312-2 (cloth);
0-88738-823-X (paper)
Printed in the United States of America

Library of Congress Cataloging-in-Publication Data

Jernazian, Ephraim K., 1890-
  [Irawunk'e chshmartut'ean. English]
  Judgment unto truth: witnessing the Armenian genocide / by Ephraim K.
Jernazian; translated by Alice Haig.
     p. cm. -- (The Zoryan Institute survivors' memoirs; no. 4)
  Translation of: Irawunk'e chshmartut'ean.
  ISBN 0-88738-312-2. -- ISBN 0-88738-823-X (pbk.)
  1. Jernazian, Ephraim K., 1890- . 2. Armenians--Turkey--Urfa--History. 3.
Armenian massacres, 1915-1923--Personal narratives. 4. Urfa (Turkey)--
History. I. Title. II. Series: Survivors' memoirs; no. 4.
DS51.U7J4713 1990
956.6'2--dc20
                                                                 89-20662
                                                                 CIP

Contents

Part IV: Prison and Release

Dedicated

to

the Armenian Martyrs

and to

the freedom and dignity

of

all peoples.

B L A C K
CONSTANTINOPLE
SAMS
AMASIA
BRUSA
S I V
ESKISHEHIR
ANKARA
YOZGAT
SIV
T U R K E Y
AFION-KARAHISAR
SMYRNA
KAISERI
ADANA
TARSUS
MERSIN
DEU
ALEX
ALEP
MEDITERRANEAN SEA
42°
36°
30°
28°
34°

ARMENIA

TORIC ARMENIA
ICIAN ARMENIA
RKISH ARMENIAN PROVINCES
VIET ARMENIA (1920)

Preface and Acknowledgments

From the day that my father, the Reverend Ephraim Jernazian, arrived in America, those who heard of his experiences in the "Old Country" were fascinated, moved, and often amazed. During his active years he would describe some of these events, in personal encounters and in public lectures. He also wrote articles for newspapers and periodicals here and abroad. Many urged him to publish them in book form in both Armenian and English.

This volume is his response. He wrote the original manuscript in Armenian and collected photographs for the book. While he was living, I had the opportunity to work with him to make sure that my English translation reflected his thoughts accurately.

I am indebted to my mother, the late Marie Hovagimian Jernazian, who reviewed the final draft of the Armenian version and made some further clarifications regarding those segments of the story of which she was a part. I am grateful to all my family who gave full support to the project in various ways, particularly to my husband whose critique of the English version was especially valuable, and to the many friends whose interest and encouragement helped keep the project alive.

Special thanks are due to the Reverend Dr. Vahan Tootikian and to Prof. Vahakn Dadrian for their review of the manuscripts and for their Introductions, the former for the Armenian version and the latter for the English version; to Dr. Hrair Dekmejian for his help in promoting the publication of the book; and finally, to Director Gerard Libaridian and the staff of the Zoryan Institute, who performed the critical step of carrying the book through to publication.

Alice Jernazian Haig

Introduction
by Vahakn Dadrian

The history of the Armenian Genocide still remains largely a compilation of survivor accounts reflecting the trauma of a nation that barely escaped extinction. That escape, narrow as it was, in no small way epitomizes a centuries-old Armenian legacy of faith and tenacity affording the miracle of survival and recuperation. Practically every survivor account is indeed testimony to the epic dimensions of a national temper in which and through which protracted suffering is harnessed and converted into resilience, allowing the victims to rebound, and to forge a will for regeneration beyond survival. The Armenian sense of tragedy as a national destiny is inextricably interwoven with a self-renewing pathos for redemption. In the unending chain of calamities, often imperiling the very survival of the nation, Armenians throughout history, but especially in recent history, have never been completely overcome by the recurrent experience of despair. The abiding residues of trauma, deeply etched in the Armenian psyche, somehow co-exist with stronger impulses of hope and vitality.

The present volume is a telling document in this respect. It is the record of what the Germans call *Erlebnis*, a lived experience, and as such a mirror image of the unabating and lethal tribulations of a nation held in bondage by oppressors gone mad and bent on genocidal destruction.

But it is much more than that. Unlike other survivors, cataloging the litany of atrocities in a narrative vein, the author presents comments and interpretations which portray him as an acute observer of intricate events. His insights and perceptions are enhanced by the benefits of decades of time and distance, during which he evidently sharpened his focus in his memoirs through retrospection and distillation.

His perspective is singularly enhanced by an asset denied to most other survivor authors. He not only had the status of a potential victim, ever vulnerable to instant annihilation in the vortex of the genocidal conflagration, but also had the distinct advantage of acquiring precious familiarity with the mind-set of the victimizers. As a chief government interpreter at Urfa, he heard, listened, eavesdropped, and occasionally was confided to, about the designs, secrets, and methods of the highest provincial authorities obeying orders from the capital of the Ottoman Empire. This position of trust

1

accorded to him by the provincial government reinforces the fact that he was neither identified with Armenian political parties nor with nationalists perceived by the authorities as being antagonistic or dangerous.

This apolitical stance, reinforced by his pervasive religiousness and pastoral calling, appears to have served him well in purging his accounts of excessive partisanship. Instead, one encounters frequent evocations of Biblical maxims as channels of lamentation and relief from despair, with only occasional lapses in outright condemnation of crimes of which he had become a witness, and on a number of occasions, a target. In brief, he had all the dubious benefits accruing to a man who finds himself in a twilight zone narrowly separating the victimizer from the victim. Marginality in status has no substitute in penetrating the frames of mind of given contestants, even when that contest may have been imposed upon the weaker by the stronger party.

The heroic defense of Urfa, the discussion of which is the centerpiece of the book, is illustrative of the point in terms of its developmental and consummative aspects. On the one hand, the reader is apprised of the growing sense of terror among the Armenians anticipating deportation and destruction and, on the other, of the machinations of a truculent government determined to find excuses, and not finding them, resorting to fabrication for its anti-Armenian measures. Here we have the classic description of the anatomy of a defensive insurrection by a small group of people who prefer to die fighting in the face of imminent annihilation. The patience of the Urfa Armenian population is extraordinary, as they endure provocation after provocation: A consecutive series of mass arrests followed by the tortures and slaughter of the community leaders; the tales of horror related by the emaciated remnants of deportee caravans passing in transit through the city; the extortions of rapacious officials; the savage killing of victims lured and trapped on solemn oaths (on the Koran) guaranteeing their safety; the serial abductions; the rapes committed in public and in broad daylight; the arrival of ex-convicts released from prisons and led by the two henchmen of the Teshkilati Mahsusa (Special Organization), namely Halil and Ahmed; the execution of Armenian deputies Vartkes and Zohrab — all these are ingredients of a pattern of incremental provocation.

Equally significant is the picture of a list of community leaders not yet arrested, who insist on giving the authorities the benefit of the doubt, who want to avoid giving the slightest excuse to them, who reject the idea of resistance and advocate compliance, and thereby impair the preparation of effective defense. The resulting discords which mark the cleavages between opposing elements — the conservative, the timid, and the clergymen on the one hand, and the young, the highly skeptical, and the intrepid, willing to fight rather than be slaughtered by the Turks, on the other — emerge in these memoirs as the pathetic symptoms of a collectivity trapped in the clutches of an inexorable foe. In such situations, prolonged dissension has historically always proved fatal, as it serves to undermine the spirit of resistance, substituting hesitation for resolve. The author vividly describes the pivotal role of leadership in the organization and execution of armed resistance, irrespective of the heavy odds involved. In this sense, the spectre of Mgrdich Yotneghparian shines like an effervescent lighthouse providing direction while illuminating. His uncanny premonition of the disaster threatening the Armenian population of Urfa, his ability to elude repeatedly the snares and traps of the authorities, his exploits against the ammunition depots and warehouses of the Ottoman military, his capacity to variably disguise himself as a Kurdish tribesman, as a Turkish officer, as an Ottoman inspector, his extraordinary presence in situations which might have caused a lesser man to panic, are all attributes of a leadership that is nothing short of legendary. In fact, in Urfa he became the savior of Armenian honor, and the architect of the valor issuing from it, ultimately dying a hero's death in the ruins of Urfa's Armenian quarter.

Counterpoised to this melodrama of life and death struggle is the picture of the chicanery, deceit, and perfidy indulged in by authorities eager to avoid battle and to resort to plain massacre after rendering the targeted victims defenseless.

The author's revelations of rampant bribery among these officials shed light on the underlying motivations of the scheme of deportation. A case in point is a detailed account of the removal of a piece of apparently incriminating evidence on the part of a member of the court martial in exchange for a large bribe. This material is a notebook containing the membership list of the Dashnag party branch in Urfa. But this evidence is anything but incriminating or insurrectional as far as the apprehensive Armenians are concerned, for it contains only the "outline of the Armenian plan of defense drawn up in the aftermath of the massacre of 1909 (in Adana)."

Turkish accounts have uniformly misrepresented such defensive plans as "separatist" and "revolutionary" designs, completely ignoring the history of antecedent massacres and the painful memories they engender in the minds of the survivors and their offspring. Urfa was particularly burdened with the ballast of such memories relative to the 1894-6 Hamidian cycle of massacres. In December 1895, during the second phase of those massacres in Urfa, eight thousand Armenians were destroyed in forty-eight hours (December 28 and 29), three thousand of them burned alive in the great Armenian cathedral where women and children had taken refuge upon the advice of the authorities who claimed to be pursuing only adult male Armenians. It is against this background that a small group of Armenians, a fraction of the total population, prepared a blueprint for defense.

The aftermath of the defense of Urfa, as chronicled by the author, is even more illuminating about the central objectives of deportations. Apart from the savagery with which decapitations of suckling babes at the altar of the Armenian church (reminiscent of the 1895 Urfa cathedral decapitations prior to its being torched) are re-enacted, government-sponsored plunder on a massive scale is set in motion under the motto of administering "the

3

abandoned goods" of the Armenians. Characterizing the deportations as an effort "to extinguish the race," nearby Aleppo's American Consul Jackson diagnoses one underlying motive as "a gigantic plundering scheme." The services of the author are needed for that scheme, too. He witnesses the unabashed thievery, embezzlement, and graft surrounding that administration of abandoned goods when translating Armenian accounts and helping prepare inventories, which are then altered to become bogus lists to suit the schemes of the officials. As far as it is known, he is also the first author to question, on valid grounds, the authenticity of American Consular Agent Leslie's suicide note that even so-called knowledgeable missionaries accepted as bona fide.

As a rule, memoirs of this genre are those of political leaders and are tinged with a penchant for self-righteousness and self-vindication. It is left to informed readers and skeptical critics to discern these elements in an overall evaluation, and to determine the scale of their incidence. Presently, the reader faces a work in which the author is mostly an observer and rarely a participant in the political aspects of the major episodes of the Turko-Armenian conflict. On the political level, his only leadership role develops in the Armistice period, when he negotiates with the British, who wanted to — and briefly did — occupy Urfa. Consequently, there is very negligible ground warranting self-vindication, if one discounts the author's repeated warnings to the timid and gullible among the Armenian community leaders that unless they prepare themselves for defense and honorable death, they are doomed to the same fate befalling the rest of the Armenian nation in Turkey, i.e., death by deportation-destruction.

The author's narration of the epic of the Urfa resistance, however brief, is perhaps the most striking feature of the book, as it correlates and blends the vantage grounds of both the Armenians, resisting, and the Turks, assaulting. In that respect alone, the volume represents a distinct contribution, while at the same time putting to the lie the claims of armchair historians and political apologists that the Urfa episode was a dastardly act of seditious rebellion by Armenian subjects sabotaging the Turkish war effort.

In conclusion, it may be stated that this volume is a unique document of historical significance, deserving the attention of not only the general public but also of students of the Armenian Genocide, perpetrated under the cover of alleged emergency wartime measures and billed as population relocations.

Part I
Early Years

1. Eclipses and Armenians

The rooftop was cold and noisy. I was numb with chill and terror, lying very still, my back against the bordering two-foot high stone wall. My older brother Luther lay stretched out beside me. Following his instructions very carefully, I kept my eyes shut tight and over and over again fervently repeated the Lord's Prayer in my native Armenian: "*Ov Hayr Mer vor yerginkun yes . . . .*"

Today as I write these words in Los Angeles, California, I am past the age of seventy-five. Then, on that rooftop in the city of Marash, Turkey, I was barely five. But that distant morning of November 18, 1895, and the events that followed remain vivid and unforgettable.

Early that morning the whole city of Marash had suddenly been filled with fire and fury. What later became known as the "Massacre of 1895" had come to our city. News of a massacre at Zeitun (about thirty miles north and slightly west of Marash) had been received about a month earlier. Since then, sensing that their turn might come soon, the Armenians in Marash kept close to home and moved about cautiously. As a child, of course, I was aware only of the extra restrictions on my outdoor play.

Once before I had heard the sounds of guns and cannon, when the moon was in eclipse. The occasion had been exciting. We went out and watched as the Turks gathered around a cannon in the street and shot salvos of balls and bullets into the sky. They were upset about the wild beast in the sky that was covering the moon and threatening to destroy the earth. The shots rang out until the moon reappeared.

This time my oldest brother Dicran (age nineteen) made sure none of us left the house. He was in a grave mood and gathered the family together in the upper room for special prayers. Family prayers were a daily routine; they gave me a sense of well-being. I vaguely remembered having had special prayers on only three previous occasions, once when Uncle Avedis died, and once each time our parents died. Illness had taken them away, and everything had been quiet on those days. No one had died today, and the town was full of noise. Why were we having special prayers instead of going outside to watch the shooting, as we did during the darkening of the moon?

My brother Luther (age sixteen) led me to the upper room. Dicran and his wife Khatoun were already there with their little baby Krikor in her lap.

My other brother Samuel (age fourteen) came soon. The din and roar outside increased. The tension and anxiety in the room disappeared as Dicran spoke and prayed. As we knelt there together, we felt a sense of closeness to each other and to God. I could not grasp all Dicran said, but I understood that the Turks would soon be coming to our house, and that they might kill us if we did not agree to be separated from Jesus. I was confused. Shooting a wild beast on the moon seemed proper, but shooting us for loving Jesus? Why? It did not seem right to ask questions. I remained silent.

The Turks did come — very soon — while we were still praying. The mob chopped down our front door, and three soldiers with guns, bolting up the stairs, broke into the room glowering fiercely. Without asking any questions, one pointed his gun directly at Dicran. Samuel stood up, stepped in front of Dicran, and pleaded, "Kill me if you have to, but spare my brother. He has a wife and a baby to look after." Dicran jumped aside and forward saying, "My brother is very young; give him a chance. Kill me if you must." The scowling intruders retorted, "Don't worry, it's no problem. We will kill you both." As the fatal shots rang out, I saw my two brothers collapse, lifeless, onto the floor. Petrified with horror and bewilderment, I clung tightly to Luther. He grasped me firmly, and instantly whisked me up through the skylight out to the roof.

We then jumped down onto the adjoining roof of the Third Armenian Evangelical Church School. Luther placed me along our wall, and he lay in front of me to protect me from gunfire. The reverberating sounds of incessant shooting and piercing shouts came at us from the street and from the rooftops, from all directions. Some of the bullets struck close. Luther's presence and the prayers gave me some comfort, but I shuddered still. The horrors of the last hour made ugly inroads upon my prayers. I wondered: What would the Turks do with Khatoun and the baby? Had the Turks reached my two sisters — three-year-old Dirouhi, who after the death of our parents had gone to live with our maternal grandmother, and my older married sister Aghavni, who lived in another part of town? What would happen to our little dog Funduk? But I was too stunned by all that I had just seen and heard to be able to think much about anything.

Suddenly the air was still. Luther was not stirring. As I cautiously lifted my head, I could see blood covering my brother, and before I could look further, I felt a rough hand grasp my shoulder. It was our Turkish neighbor: "Come, I will take you to our home." Frantically I struggled, and repeatedly cried in vain, "I love Jesus! I won't be a Turk! You killed my brothers. Kill me!" The Turk took me to his wife and told her to feed me. But how could I put a single morsel into my mouth? I passed the night trembling and shedding silent tears.

At daybreak a town crier announced, "The purge is over. Every Turk who has Armenian women and children must take them to Jernazian's church." The Armenian Episcopal Church was called "Jernazian's church" because my uncle Stephen had established it and was pastor there. The Turk who had taken me home the night before took my hand and led me to my uncle's church. As I walked, I was mainly preoccupied with avoiding all the rubble, especially the bits of broken glass, because I was not wearing shoes. They had been left at home when we escaped the day before. (Since streets were unpaved and floors were covered with rugs, shoes had to be removed on entering a house. We followed this custom, and I had my shoes off while in our upper room. There was no opportunity to put them on when Luther rushed me out.)

As we arrived at the church, I was filled with new horror when I saw the hundreds of wounded men, crying children, and distraught women crowded into the worship hall. The Turk who had taken me there promptly called out in a loud voice, "Who is here from the Jernazian family? I have brought their little boy. Let them come and claim him." To my great relief, Khatoun came forth at once and took me beside her. My brothers' assassins, who had abducted her, had brought her and baby Krikor unharmed to the church when the town crier had announced the end of the massacre. The Turk who brought me to the church left disappointed, for his plan to adopt me and claim the Jernazian properties was thwarted. It was customary in those times for Turks to adopt Armenian orphans, take over their inheritance, then either kill the children or raise them as Moslems.

Khatoun and I cried and cried until we were exhausted. The plight of the people in that church was sorrowful beyond description. Most of the women had seen their husbands killed and their homes vandalized and looted. They had no help from any source and not a shred of hope. Death seemed preferable to life under those conditions. That night in the church seemed like a year.

Early the following morning I heard a familiar voice. Was it coming from Heaven? It was the voice of my older sister. She was there in person, looking for us: "I am Aghavni, daughter of Krikor Effendi. Is there anyone here from the Jernazian family?" (Effendi was a Turkish title of respect by which my father was addressed.) Greatly relieved, I immediately ran to her and clutched her. Khatoun followed closely with the baby. My sister's neighbor, a Circassian captain, Hassan Effendi, had taken her family and about ten other Armenian families into his mansion to protect them. He had also sent his soldiers to guard the homes of those families.

With the consent of a Turkish guard at the church, Aghavni took us to her home. For a long time we sat there dejected and bewildered, my sister holding her little nephew in her lap. Our eyes were brimming with tears. We could not understand why these horrible things had happened.

The day after we were reunited, my sister and her husband Nazaret, taking me with them, went to our home. When we entered the upper room, we saw the bodies of Dicran and Samuel still there, lying in dried pools of blood. Our little dog Funduk was standing guard and would let no one come near the bodies. He must have had no food for three days. As soon as he saw me, he ran to me and, whining mournfully, jumped up to me. We took Funduk with us — loyal, affectionate Funduk. Nazaret hired two men to bury my two brothers temporarily in the yard of our home. The Armenian cemetery was outside the city limits; Armenians were being confined to the city and could not use the cemetery.

As for the body of my brother Luther, it was nowhere to be seen. We could not find it on the roof or anywhere else. For one whole month every time we saw a corpse, we examined it to see if it might be Luther. We searched and inquired everywhere but with no success. Grief remained heavy in our hearts.

Then one day a knock at the door brought a friend of ours, a tinsmith, who announced, "I have good news for you — very good news!" We were amazed. In those evil, cursed days, what possible good news could there be? Our friend continued, "Your brother is alive. He is in the Turkish hospital. Go to him quickly. He is waiting for you." Our friend had been called to the hospital to repair a stove and, while there, had recognized my brother. We went immediately to the hospital and, seeing at least one of our brothers actually alive, gave thanks to God. There was no limit to our joy. We learned that Luther had received five bullet wounds. As he lay near death, he had been discovered by a Turkish captain on an inspection tour of the Third Armenian Evangelical Church next to our house. The captain, a friend of Luther's, had ordered his soldiers to transport my brother to the hospital at once.

How was such friendship possible? This ironical situation was not unique. In the Ottoman Empire in times of peace, Turks and Armenians living side by side often had friendly relationships. Being forced into the position of second class subjects for several centuries, the Armenians had learned to cope with discrimination as a way of life. With ingenuity and hard work, for the most part they led useful and resignedly contented lives. The Turkish people, for their part, enjoyed their position of official superiority. Being dependent for many economic necessities on their Armenian subjects, the Turks willingly accepted the services of the *giavoors* (infidels), as the Christians were called, and maintained a tolerant attitude while exploiting them. The sultan was the religious and political head of the Empire. The Turkish Moslem population unquestioningly obeyed their chief. Disobedience meant death. Triggered by various motives, the sultan periodically decreed a *jihad* (holy war) against the infidel Christians. Then friendship was instantly suspended between Turk and Armenian. As soon as the sultan decided to stop the slaughter, friendships were resumed. So the Turkish captain had participated in the massacre, but now he performed this act of kindness for his Armenian friend, my brother Luther.

My sister obtained permission from the medical chief at the hospital to take Luther to her home, where she nursed him for many months until he recovered adequately. Thus Aghavni, Luther, and I survived the Massacre of 1895. Khatoun and Baby Krikor joined her family, who had likewise escaped death. Dirouhi and my maternal grandmother also survived; they had found refuge in the Catholic church. But my grandfather and my brothers Dicran and Samuel were killed. My Uncle Stephen was also murdered, and his wife, Aunt Yepros, died when she received the news. The story of Uncle Stephen's martyrdom became a legend in the city. He and several of his church officers had been seized and brought out from a basement where they had gathered. He was taken aside while his colleagues were killed. Reverend Stephen was then brought back and shown the mutilated bodies of his friends. He was offered a "special privilege": "We know you are a good man and great. Become a Moslem and we will spare your life."

Three times they offered, and three times he refused, saying, "Do not force me to deny my Lord. I am ready to die with my friends." His wish was granted. As he died, he prayed forgiveness for his murderers. The Turks who carried out the assignment to kill my uncle and his colleagues related the incidents themselves, with a bit of awe but hardly with remorse.

2. Fragments from a Lost History

O ur loss of property during the Massacre of 1895 was extensive. The family import-export business and our olive ranch were destroyed. Our home was emptied of all its contents, even to the ashes in the hearth.

One day after the massacre a Turkish neighbor of ours named Osman, for whom my father had done many favors, came to my sister's home and said, "Aghavni Hanum [a title of respect for women], by the sultan's orders I took part in the massacres and plunder. I got a number of things from your father's home. Please say *konshu, halal olsun* [neighbor, bless you!] so I can have a clear conscience and enjoy what I've taken." Needless to say, my sister would not give him the satisfaction. Instead, she said, "Osman, with what kind of conscience can you expect me to say halal when you've been such an ingrate, a thief, and a murderer? No, no.-I have to say Osman, *haram olsun* [curse you!] for what you did."

In those trying times my sister Aghavni, who was twenty-four years old, courageously endured our endless troubles and was a source of strength to all of us. She and her husband Nazaret had two children about my age. They took in my wounded brother and myself as well. We began to rebuild our lives.

Of all our losses, the one irreplaceable item was a family history my father had written. With it was lost much information I might have had about my background. Aghavni and Luther told me a few fragments, but I was not with them very much when I was old enough to understand such matters. When I did see them, they were reluctant to talk about the family past. Perhaps the heartache was too great, or perhaps the problems of the day were all we had time to talk about.

One story which Luther told me I remember very well, since it shows how early in life God's protective hand was upon me — even from the day I was baptized as an infant. At birth I was named Sarkis. On the morning of my baptismal day, during family prayers before church, the Bible reading was from the 48th chapter of Genesis in which Jacob blesses his grandsons Ephraim and Manasseh, giving Ephraim, the younger, a special blessing. My father suddenly said, "I want to name my youngest son Effrayim (the Turkish form of Ephraim) that he shall be specially blessed." And so it was.

A number of times throughout the critical years of persecutions, having the name of Effrayim saved me from interrogation by Turkish authorities and from certain harassment or even death. When asked, "What is your name?" if I had replied, "Sarkis," that obviously non-Moslem name would have assured further questioning. Effrayim, being a name used also by Turks, elicited no further probes. I was allowed to pass on. (Surnames were not required in those days.)

Other relatives and friends have told me a little about my family. The martyred Stephen was my father's oldest brother. He had been one of the charter members of the First Evangelical Church of Marash, established in 1854. He was a graduate of Bebek American College of Constantinople and of the Marash Theological Seminary. His first pastorate was in Egypt at Cairo, where he was also tutor of a son of Boghos Nubar Pasha, the internationally known Armenian philanthropist and statesman. In 1885, having returned to Marash, Uncle Stephen established the first Episcopal church there and served until the tragedy of 1895. Noting the similarity between the Episcopal Church and the Armenian Apostolic Church, he had become an Episcopalian. He thought adopting this denomination might lead to the reconciliation of the Armenian Apostolic Church and the Armenian Protestant community.

My father Krikor was the youngest of the brothers. He and his other brother Avedis were partners in business, successful merchants in the import-export trade. They were active lay stewards in the First Evangelical Church of Marash. Later my father transferred to the Second Evangelical Church, where I was baptized by the Reverend Aharon Shirajian. Uncle Avedis's wife, Shamira, was a sister of the Reverend Hampartsoum Ashjian, a professor at the Marash Theological Seminary and pastor at Aintab, Adana, and Konia (Iconium). Neither of my uncles had any children.

One suburb of Marash was called "Jernaz(ian) District," in honor of my father who was the first to obtain olive trees and produce olives in Marash. Having brought seedlings from Kilis, a town about one hundred miles south of Marash, he planted them two miles outside the city. Many were skeptical at first, and some ridiculed the idea. But the results were successful and encouraged others to try. Before long, olives and olive oil were fast becoming a substantial source of revenue for the city.

Uncle Avedis died in 1892 as a result of unsuccessful surgery. My mother, née Mariam Shamlian, died of cholera the following year when I was three. My father died a year later, of a broken heart — I was told.

My father had one sister; I do not know when or how she died. Thirty-two years after the Massacre of 1895, I discovered her son-in-law, Steve Arabian, and his two daughters as parishioners in our church at Troy, New York. He had no further information about the Jernazian family. He was a widower. His wife, my cousin, had heard that we were to come to Troy and eagerly awaited our arrival. She became ill and died just before we reached the city.

My only close relative with whom I could keep in touch after coming to America was my mother's brother, Astor Shamlian. He was very fond of his sister and visited her grave almost daily for a year after she died. He told me that my maternal grandfather, Hagop Shamlian, had died young. Ten years later my grandmother Pambuk Anna had married a Catholic, who died in the Massacre of 1895. *Pambuk* is the Turkish word for cotton. My grandmother acquired the name because of her soft, fair complexion. I have a very hazy recollection of her. I never knew my other grandparents, and I know nothing more about any of them.

3. A Lion and Forty Eyes

B efore going on with my personal story, let me describe the city of my birth. Marash was a fascinating place in which to grow up. As we played in the yard or walked along the streets, we found ancient relics. All around us were reminders of a glorious and mysterious past, including Hittite ruins from as far back as the second millennium BC. One of these antiquities that especially impressed me as a young boy was a large statue of a Hittite lion atop the main gate of the fortress in the center of the city. We boys used to make up our own versions of what the many inscriptions on the lion meant. That statue is now in an archeological museum in Constantinople (Istanbul). In 1966 I saw it in Los Angeles as part of a travelling exhibition. The "Lion of Marash" brought back many memories.

One of the oldest cities in Asia Minor, Marash is first recorded in history around the twelfth century BC as Marqasi, capital of the Hittite kingdom of Gurgun. In the ninth century BC it was part of an alliance with the Urartian kings. In 711 BC Gurgun was occupied by the Assyrian King Sargon II, and Marqasi remained under Assyrian rule until the Scythian invasion followed shortly by the Persian conquest. In 333 BC Marash came under Alexander the Great, and after his death passed under Seleucid rule. Then came Roman rule (when the city was known as Germanicia), followed successively by Byzantines, Arabs, Armenians, and Crusaders. Then, after being occupied from the end of the fourteenth century by Seljuks and Egyptians, by the sixteenth century it finally passed into the hands of the Ottoman Turks. Many Armenians still call Marash Kermanig, its Roman name.

Marash is situated at the foot of the Akhorisu Mountains, a part of the Taurus chain. It enjoys a varied climate and fertile soil. I remember the abundant flow of clear spring water that came from the base of the mountains at the northeastern part of the city. A reservoir called Kurk Geuz (Forty Eyes) supplied the entire valley by a system of tile pipes. I remember, also, the thriving grain, fruit, and vegetables. Our house was on a hill overlooking a triple-terraced garden with many fruit trees (apricot, peach, two kinds of cherry, fig, and white, red, and black mulberry) and grapevines as well as a variety of flowers along the side of which flowed a sparkling stream. The roses were very fragrant and delighted the schoolgirls when distributed among them from time to time.

15

The population of Marash as I knew it in 1913 was about 75,000: 45,000 Turks and 30,000 Armenians. Other nationalities had very small representation. Almost all the businesses and crafts were conducted by Armenians. Likewise, physicians, pharmacists, and attorneys were, with few exceptions, Armenians. As for the Turks, they were government officials, farmers, shepherds, and laborers who demanded high pay for little work. Turkish tradesmen consisted of blacksmiths and tanners.

There were both Turkish and Armenian schools in Marash. The Turks provided no schools for girls. Some of the Turkish schools were administered by Moslem priests. Boys who attended these schools barely learned how to read and write. They were taught the mechanics of reading the Koran in Arabic but could not comprehend or discuss what they read. Other Turkish schools were public schools administered by the government, tuition free. Very few attended these. Those who did prepared for government jobs.

Armenian schools had been established centuries ago throughout Armenia in connection with the churches. A number of institutions of higher learning had been maintained in cities and monasteries. They graduated able clergy, philosophers, teachers, and writers. Turkish persecutions since the Middle Ages, especially of the cultured citizens, had greatly handicapped educational activities among Armenians. In the 19th century American missionaries to Turkey had no success in efforts to convert the Turks but found a promising field in helping to fill educational needs among Armenians. The missionaries established high schools and colleges in predominantly Armenian towns, and a university at Beirut. These proved to be a great blessing, a means for thousands of eager young people to receive higher education and to come into contact with other Christian cultures.

In the last seven centuries Marash had been one of the largest centers of Armenian population in Cilicia — a region of Asia Minor enclosed by the Taurus Mountains along the west and north, and the Amanus Range along the east, its shoreline extending around the northeastern corner of the Mediterranean Sea from Seleucia at the west to Antioch at the east. The missionaries, therefore, chose Marash to establish a girls' college and a theological seminary there. Armenian elementary and secondary schools were maintained by the churches. When I lived in Marash, six Armenian Apostolic churches served 20,000 members; four Protestant churches served 5,000 members; and two Catholic churches, one with Latin clergy and one with Armenian clergy, served another 5,000. Protestantism and Catholicism were established in Marash in the middle of the nineteenth century. The first Protestant church was organized in 1854 at the Patpatian home with sixteen members. The first Catholic church began in 1857. The Apostolic Church was, of course, the official national church of Armenia, established in AD 301. Christianity itself had entered from the time of the apostles Thaddeus and Bartholomew.

4. Narrow Escapes at Ebenezer and Ak-Soo

T he Massacre of 1895 left hundreds of orphans and wounded in Marash and in the villages nearby. To care for them, German and American missionaries opened hospitals and orphanages. Mrs. L. O. Lee, daughter of Dr. Cyrus B. Hamlin of Constantinople (one of the first American missionaries to Turkey) and close friend of our family, was director of the boys' orphanage named Ebenezer (stone of help — from I Samuel 7:12) and of a girls' orphanage. The home of a wealthy Turk, Dede Pasha, next to the American missionary headquarters, had been bought and converted for use as the boys' orphanage. Mrs. Lee convinced my sister Aghavni to let me enter Ebenezer where I would have more opportunities than at home.

The government gave each boy, upon entry into the orphanage, a copy of a certificate of citizenship stating the place and year of birth. Mine said "Marash, 1306." This is the Turkish date, which is calculated from Mohammed's pilgrimage from Mecca to Medina in AD 622. By the Christian calendar, 1306 becomes 1890. Just as our calendar refers to years before and after the birth of Christ, the Moslem calendar refers to years *hichretden evel* (before the pilgrimage) and *hichretden sonra* (after the pilgrimage).* Since all our family records had been destroyed in 1895, I would otherwise have had no official birth certificate. As for the month, my uncle Astor told me that I was born toward the end of November.

At Ebenezer I received good care — physical, moral, and spiritual — as did eventually hundreds of other orphans. Every day we had prayer and Bible study sessions. On Sundays we attended morning and afternoon services at the Armenian Evangelical churches in the city. Sunday evenings all the American and German orphanages had their respective joint meetings. We attended the American service regularly.

Our educational needs were also well provided. From Monday through Friday we attended the schools administered by the Evangelical churches.

---

* The difference between 1890 and 1306 appears to be 584 years instead of 622. The figures are compatible when an adjustment is made for the fact that 1890 is based on a solar calendar and 1306 is based on a shorter lunar calendar.

Most of the boys learned a trade after finishing elementary school. A few of us went on to colleges and universities. We college-bound students also learned manual skills. At Ebenezer I learned bookbinding. During summers I learned shoemaking from my brother-in-law Nazaret and from Luther.

My father, through his trade contacts, had brought the first shoe-stitching machine to Marash for his son-in-law Nazaret. When Luther recovered from his wounds, he learned shoemaking and worked with Nazaret for a time. Later he opened his own shop and sewed new shoes only. Although the family import-export business had been destroyed, Luther was able to keep the title to our family home. He rented it out to Turkish government officials. After he was married, he lived in the front section of the home and continued to rent out the rear. He developed a successful shoemaking business and bought a vineyard, where he had a summer home. Luther and his wife Makruhi had two daughters, Marie and Lydia. Nazaret and Aghavni had three sons, Garabed, Krikor, and Samuel, and three daughters, Armenouhi, Maria, and Aghavni. By the time I left for college they had all settled down to a normal existence.

Of my experiences at the orphanage, two stand out in my memory because on those occasions I came very close to death. The first was in 1902, while about twenty of us were in the baths in the center of the building. The fire which provided our hot water also heated the ovens in the adjacent bakery. One afternoon after the fire in the oven had been put out, some wood had been placed in it to dry overnight for use the next day. A few live embers in the rear went unnoticed. It did not take long for these to ignite the wood. As one piece burst into flames, it was thrown out onto the wooden floor. (This oven was a built-in stone furnace with an open front.) The flames spread rapidly and came toward us. We were frightened into an instant dash out of the baths. We barely made it out of the building and saved our skins.

The other narrow escape came the following year while I was traveling from Marash to Aintab for eye surgery. At the age of two I had lost the sight of my left eye as the result of an infection. In 1903 this eye was causing me much chronic pain. I was, therefore, being sent to the American Missionary Hospital at Aintab for examination and treatment. There surgical removal of the eye and replacement by an artificial eye gave me permanent relief and enabled me to carry on a normal life.

The road to Aintab at one point crossed the Ak-Soo River. There was no bridge, and most of the time horses had no trouble going through the water. But when we arrived at the crossing, we found that this spring the river had overflowed and was much fuller and wider than usual. We had no choice but to ride through, hoping that our horses could still get us across safely. About half way across, my horse suddenly tripped, and the next moment we were being carried downstream by the rushing current. I went under water up to my mouth, managing to hang onto the horse and trying hard to breathe yet avoid swallowing water. Once more I prayed desperately. Before we were too far out of reach, a guide came to our rescue and helped us cross the rest of the way. (Since my early childhood the Turkish government had been collecting taxes from the Armenians of Marash to build several miles of road outside of the city as well as a bridge over the Ak-Soo River. When I was twenty-four years old, I again crossed the Ak-Soo River on my way to Aintab, and still neither the road nor the bridge had been built. In 1919, when the British occupied Marash temporarily, they built, within two months, several miles of road and a beautiful bridge across the Ak-Soo.)

The person who arranged for my medical care at Aintab was Miss Agnes Salmond, who became director of the orphanage in 1898. Like Mrs. Lee before her, she showed a personal concern for each of us. Her kindness and wisdom provided many happy experiences for all of us who lived there.

Miss Salmond was born in 1846 in the city of Kirkintilloch, Scotland, of devout parents. When she learned of the tribulations of the Armenians in 1895, she dedicated herself to helping Armenian orphans and widows. In 1896 she went to Smyrna under auspices of the British organization "Friends of Armenia," and after working there two years, she came to Marash as general director of the orphanages. She also helped many widows, arranging for them to produce various kinds of fine handwork which found a wide market in England and America as "Ebenezer Handwork." She worked unceasingly. In addition to carrying on her numerous duties at hand, she wrote many letters to find sponsors from England, Holland, and America. When in 1915 the Turkish government once again began to deport and massacre Armenians, and she saw the children of the orphans she had cared for becoming orphans or being killed, her tired, sensitive soul could no longer bear the burden. Exhausted, she returned to England. Even in her weak and ill condition she prayed for her surviving orphans and extended whatever help she could. Miss Salmond closed her eyes on December 10, 1940, at the age of ninety-four, to receive her due reward from her Heavenly Father. Even to the end she continued to show a genuine interest in our lives, writing letters of encouragement and offering support when needed.

5. Tarsus, the Renowned City of Cilicia

I n 1904, upon my graduation from the Marash Academy, Miss Salmond sent me to Zeitun for a year to teach at the Armenian Evangelical School there. That year I grew both physically and spiritually. The people of Zeitun inspired me with their fortitude and courageous resistance to Turkish attacks. The experience proved valuable for me in later years.

In the fall of 1905 Miss Salmond sent me, together with three of my classmates, to college at St. Paul's in Tarsus. I was very happy as a student there, but that winter I became seriously ill. The doctor was out of town, and my condition was critical. When Miss Salmond heard the news, she immediately transferred me back to Marash where, with proper medical care, I recovered in a few days. During the rest of that school year I remained at the orphanage and taught evening classes for the boys who were trade apprentices during the daytime. For the summer, my friend Mihran Gumushian invited me to stay with his family in Lampron, in the Taurus Mountains north of Tarsus near the source of the Cydnus River. I was received very cordially and enjoyed both working and relaxing with the Gumushians.

In September of 1906 I returned to college at Tarsus as a sub-freshman. I had not yet studied French, which was required for full freshman status. Within a year I was eligible to enter the freshman class. The one note of sadness at this time was that my grandmother had died, and soon afterward my young sister Dirouhi. I do not know the details of my grandmother's death. My sister had been transferred in 1898 to a German missionary orphanage in Smyrna where she was safe for several years. She was fourteen when she fell victim to tuberculosis, contracted from the house mother. A photographic miniature of Dirouhi, which she sent me, and a piece of her handwork, which Aghavni gave me, are very precious mementos I have been able to preserve. Dirouhi joined the members of the family who had gone to Heaven. I stayed on at Tarsus and plunged into the mainstream of life at school and in the community.

For centuries Tarsus, where St. Paul's College was established, was the most famous city in Cilicia. St. Paul calls it "the renowned city of Cilicia" (Acts 21:39). In the first century BC Strabo proclaimed Tarsus superior to Athens and Alexandria as a center for philosophical studies. Cicero, as governor of Cilicia, lived in Tarsus in 50 BC.

Tarsus is ten miles away from the Mediterranean Sea, eighty feet above sea level. North of the city begin rolling hills which rise to the Taurus Mountains thirty miles away. All year round these mountains provide an unusually beautiful setting with their snow-capped peaks. The plains of Tarsus have very fertile alluvial soil. I remember the cotton and grain crops, which were the chief products of the city, and especially the fields of wheat and barley which grew as tall as people. Fruits and vegetables were plentiful, as in Marash. In Tarsus the Cydnus River, flowing through the center of the city, provided ample water for homes and gardens. I remember, also, a small waterfall just outside the city, which provided additional scenic beauty.

Among Christians, Tarsus has significance as the birthplace of St. Paul. Among Armenians it has double significance, not only as St. Paul's birthplace but also as a political and cultural center of the Cilician Armenian kingdom. Here, on January 6, 1199, in the Church of Holy Wisdom, the first Armenian king of Cilicia was crowned — King Levon I.

The city of Tarsus was founded about 2000 BC by Ionian colonists and became highly prosperous. It was an important cultural and commercial link between East and West. As a Cilician city, Tarsus has a history similar in general to that of Marash. After Assyrian and Persian control from the eighth to the fourth century BC, Tarsus, like the rest of Cilicia, was conquered by Alexander the Great and passed into the hands of Seleucids, then Romans, Byzantines, Arabs, Armenians, and Crusaders. During the Roman era, the Armenian King Dicran the Great, Tigranes II, occupied Tarsus from 83 to 63 BC. For about two centuries from AD 1180 Tarsus was part of the kingdom of Cilician Armenia. After Seljuk and Egyptian invasions beginning at the end of the fourteenth century, Cilicia passed into the hands of Ottoman Turks in the beginning of the sixteenth century, and Tarsus lost its people and its glory. The city, which at one time had been a thriving metropolis, in 1914 had a population of barely twenty-five thousand. About five thousand of these were Armenians who struggled against great odds to rejuvenate the town. In the Massacre of 1915 these, too, were annihilated.

In Tarsus, as in Marash, historical reminders and ruins were all around us. I remember a huge gate left from an old castle, which the Turks were tearing down. A British archeologist succeeded in saving the gate from destruction. But the Turkish government would not allow any archeological digging.

One historical event was of special interest to us students at St. Paul's. In 41 BC, when Antony established his headquarters at Tarsus and summoned Cleopatra from Egypt intending to humiliate her, she sailed up the waters of the Cydnus River with all her retinue in a barge with golden canopy and silver oars and purple sails. In dazzling splendor she greeted Antony and captivated him. On the spot where they met, now called Goezlik Kooleh, St. Paul's College with its five buildings, large and small, was established.

21

6. St. Paul and Young Turks

T he founder and first president of St. Paul's College was an Armenian, the Reverend Harutiun Jenanian. Because of his dynamic evangelism and practical achievements, he was popularly called "the Mr. Moody of Cilicia." He began his career by studying two years at the Marash Theological Seminary, then continued his studies in America at the Union Theological Seminary of New York. On Sundays he attended the Fifth Avenue Presbyterian Church. There he met the philanthropist Colonel Elliott Shepard, an attorney and editor of *The Mail and Express*, whose wife was the daughter of William H. Vanderbilt and granddaughter of Cornelius Vanderbilt, the distinguished railroad, steamship, and financial tycoon and philanthropist. Reverend Jenanian brought to Colonel Shepard's attention the great need for a college in the land of St. Paul, in the city of Tarsus, to serve many studious Armenian young people there. Colonel Shepard was sympathetic and promised to donate $5,000 a year for the purpose and, upon his death, to will $100,000 as a trust fund for the school. In 1887, having graduated from Union Theological Seminary, Reverend Jenanian returned to Tarsus and the following year founded a school which was named after himself. For six years he served as president and personally taught several courses. In 1893, having brought the school to full collegiate status, he transferred the administration and the funds to the American Congregational Board of Foreign Missions, and moved to Konia where he founded another Jenanian College.

The Missionary Board changed the name of the college at Tarsus to St. Paul's College and elected a board of trustees that was exclusively American. They retained the academy, or pre-collegiate division of the school, with which Jenanian had started out, and invited as the new president for the whole complex Dr. Thomas Davidson Christie, one of the professors at the Marash Theological Seminary, who was very sympathetic toward the Armenian people. He served as president for twenty-five years. He and his gracious wife Carmelita were like a father and mother who took genuine care of the students. Dr. Christie was extremely pleased when we called him "Papa."

When I entered St. Paul's, I planned to become an engineer. Combining this interest with my hobby of carpentry, I spent many hours of my free time

in the construction of a precise scale model of the administration building. I
also continued to bind books and helped in the gardening. We had a varied
extra-curricular program as well as a curriculum patterned after those of
colleges in the United States. I participated in dramatic productions, public
speaking, college choir, and orchestra. I was given ten lessons on the flute
and permitted to teach myself violin. How proud I was when I was able to
buy my own flute and violin! I can still remember what a delightful time I
had the day I was placed in charge of instruments. I tried them all and took
good care of them for a year.

In the summer of 1907 I stayed at the home of my friend Sampson
Marashlian in Adana, a city about twenty miles east of Tarsus, and worked
at the Turpani factory weaving white muslin. The next school year was
smooth and uneventful. During the first part of the summer of 1908 my
friend Abraham Mangouney and I worked in Adana painting the interior of
the new, government-administered Turkish college buildings. Later another
friend, Serop Basmajian, joined us, and we painted the interior of our own
college auditorium in Tarsus. Toward the end of this job I had one more
close encounter with death. Serop, thinking that the scaffolding on which I
was standing was secure, stepped on the same board. Suddenly the board
broke, I fell, and the paint in my pail poured directly over my head. Serop
was unharmed, but I became unconscious. My breathing became labored.
When the doctor came and examined me, he told my friends that there was
not much hope for me but that they should continue to put ice on my head. In
the morning I began to revive, but it was difficult for me to move my head; in
fact, my whole body was stiff. The boys who were caring for me, overjoyed,
embraced me: "Yeprem (Armenian form of Effrayim), thank God, you're
alive!"

When school opened in the fall of 1908, optimism pervaded the
Armenian community. The Young Turk reformers and the Ittihad ve
Terakki (Committee of Union and Progress) had succeeded. The
Constitution had been restored. (At the beginning of his rule in 1876 the
Sultan Abdul Hamid had proclaimed the Constitution as a gesture to stave
off European pressures for reform. He had never put it into practice and had
thrown it out two years later. He continued his sadistic policies, which
culminated in the Massacres of 1894-6.) Turks and Armenians together
now shouted, "Liberty, Fraternity, Equality!" Discrimination and persecution would end. Turkey would start on the road to modernization and
democracy. Armenian leaders had cooperated with the Young Turks in
bringing about the reforms and looked forward to continued cooperation,
peace, and progress.

By the next spring this optimism was shaken. We could not know at the
time just why a massacre erupted. But, beginning at Adana on March 31,
groups of frenzied mobs attacked Armenians all over Cilicia and northern
Syria. Soldiers who were supposed to stop the murderers joined them
instead. Within the month over thirty thousand Armenians had been
massacred. The government admitted no responsibility for the killings,

conducted token trials, passed mock sentences, gave token compensation for destroyed property — chiefly to American property — and closed the issue. The following August the Ittihadists (political party of the Young Turks) still maintained a semblance of cooperation by signing a pact of friendship with the Armenian Dashnak political leaders.

The Young Turks had split into two factions, one favoring equal consideration for all citizens, the other intending to suppress all non-Turkish elements. The latter group won out and launched a fanatical policy of Pan-Turkism. Their slogan was "Turkey for the Turks" and their methods produced violent persecutions worse than any the sultans had ordered. The massacre of 1909 was just a preview of things to come. At a congress of Ittihadists in Salonika begun October 31, 1910, a final resolution was adopted to exterminate all non-Turkish elements as soon as conditions were favorable for such a drastic action. This resolution formed the basis for the full-scale Genocide begun in 1915.

At Tarsus the second week of April, 1909, we suspected nothing. During spring vacation Dr. Christie and two of his assistants, Herbert Gibbons and Miner Rogers (Dr. Christie's son-in-law), went to Adana for the fiftieth annual missions meeting. An Armenian ministers' retreat was being held there at the same time. We were awaiting good news out of Adana. But the three men did not return when expected. Instead, a group of frenzied *bashi-bozouks* (irregulars) poured into town off the train from Adana. They were joined by local mobs and launched a full-scale, savage attack on the Armenians of Tarsus. Regular soldiers joined in the looting, burning, raping, and killing. Hundreds of Armenians fled to our campus, which was next to the Armenian quarter. Mrs. Christie rose heroically to the needs of the day. She refused the consular invitation to evacuate to Mersin: "I prefer to die with my students and the Armenian people than to hand them over to the pitiless Turk and save myself." Raising the American flag above the campus, she gave refuge to over three thousand Armenians. Everyone who was able, students and staff alike, assisted in every way possible.

In one day, the whole Armenian quarter in Tarsus became a shambles, and all its inhabitants were either killed or found refuge at St. Paul's. During the massacre the fire was raging so violently that sometimes the winds blowing toward the college carried sparks to the high balcony of the administration building. When I saw the danger, I brought pails of water and, lying on the floor of the balcony, put out each spark as it fell near me. Sometimes bits of timber fell. The Turks, seeing me from a distance, shot at me several times. Once more, by God's grace, I remained unharmed.

When the Turks discovered that no more Armenians were to be found in the city, they surrounded the college complex, brought up fire-extinguishing machines, and filled them with kerosene instead of water so that they might at one stroke burn up the buildings and all the people who had sought refuge there. We were then ready fodder for fire and sword. But we were saved at the last moment when word arrived from the Young Turks in Constantinople that the massacre should stop. The so-called reformers followed the sultan's pattern. The massacre stopped as suddenly as it had started; no one knew why. The final orgy was thus put off for six years.

The day after the massacre at Tarsus, Dr. Christie and Herbert Gibbons returned. Miner Rogers was not with them; he had been killed at Adana. Other American missionaries and almost all the Armenian ministers, who were especially marked for death, had been killed.

Although the massacre at Tarsus had lasted less than one week, illness and numerous problems of restoration continued to demand attention for some time afterward. For two weeks Mrs. Christie and her staff waited on the sick and the little children both night and day. People who had found refuge on campus were afraid to leave. How could they be sure some new trap was not set for them? At that time the cotton fields of the sheikh of the Fellah tribe of Arabs were in need of weeding. (He had given refuge to five hundred Armenians during the attack on the Armenian quarter.) Several of us students decided to volunteer for the weeding. We received permission from Dr. Christie and together with several refugees went out to work in the fields for a week. When we returned safely, everyone knew that the danger was over and willingly left the campus to start life anew.

Among those who had found refuge at St. Paul's during the attack were about fifty orphans and several widows who were to go to the German orphanage in Marash. They needed escorts for the trip. Being an orphan myself, I readily volunteered. Two other boys from Marash also volunteered. We accompanied the group on the train and saw them safely to their destination, returning within a week, in time to resume classes for the spring term.

One of the widows in this group was Azniv Salisian, a young expectant bride whose husband of a year had just been killed in the Adana massacre. Her father, the Reverend Markar Calusdian, and her older brother Robert had been martyred at Hamidiye en route to the church convention in Adana. Her mother had died a natural death two years earlier. Her uncle from Marash had sent for her to go there for the safe birth of her child. On the trip we called her "Little Mother" and were especially solicitous for her comfort. Neither of us could know then that almost forty years later my daughter was to marry her nephew.

7. The Turning Point of a Lifetime

T he aftermath of the massacre of 1909 proved to be a turning point in my life. A serious shortage of Armenian pastors had been created by the murders at the Adana retreat. When school reopened in the fall, a call was extended for replacements. Several of us at Tarsus answered this call and gave up our other intended careers to enter the ministry.

The previous summer, I was still an engineering student and took a job which provided an excellent opportunity to gain firsthand experience in that field. I worked as an assistant for an Austrian engineer, whom we called Monsieur J., in his work of surveying for the Bagdad Railroad. Although I did not stay in engineering, the experience gave me new and valuable insights.

The summer of 1910 was an inspirational one. I returned to Marash, stayed with my brother Luther for a while, then spent the rest of the summer with one of my college teachers, Sarkis Antablian, hiking through the mountains and valleys of Cilicia. How exhilarating! To explore the untold beauties of God's creation — freely and away from places where there was constant fear of being ambushed by madmen. Cilicia is a region of great natural beauty. A popular Armenian song — "I long to see my Cilicia" — even today brings nostalgic memories of that summer.

In the spring of 1911, two months before my graduation, I received a second call. This time I was called for military service and was not so ready to accept. My turn was bound to come, and I wanted to do my duty as a citizen, but it was difficult to think of dying for a government antagonistic toward my faith and my people. I had no choice. A Turkish soldier escorted me to draft headquarters in Tarsus. To help lessen the strain, some of my friends brought me blankets to make my stay overnight at the headquarters more comfortable. The next morning the whole student body and faculty (about 150 altogether), with Dr. Christie's permission, came to see me off as I was boarding the train to Mersin (a seaport about fifteen miles southwest of Tarsus) for processing. I can still remember how my friend Diran Topjian tried to give me moral support as he pressed a *mejid* (one dollar) into my hand: "Don't let death scare you, Yeprem. Since you have won so many hearts, you can go with confidence. Everyone is praying for you." My music teacher gave me a recommendation for assignment to an army band.

Dr. Christie sent one of the faculty, the Reverend Aram Bagdikian, to Mersin to ask for deferment for me, at least until graduation. He was told that deferment could be granted only at Adana, our next stop.

At Adana I received help from the Reverend Hampartsoum Ashjian, Uncle Avedis's brother-in-law and protégé. My uncle had invited him at the age of fifteen to help in the Jernazian import-export business, then had supported him through Aintab College (1884) and Marash Theological Seminary (1889). Reverend Ashjian attended Yale Divinity School from 1894 to 1897. Having been ordained by the American Congregational Council in 1899, he returned to Turkey to serve his people. In 1909 he was serving in Adana. Sensing that violence against the Armenians was coming again, he had vainly tried to convince the Turkish officials of Adana, who respected him highly, to prevent that massacre. They had not changed their plans, but they had spared his life. Afterwards he had heroically spoken out in protest and had succeeded in foiling a plan to blame the Armenians for the massacre. Such token trials, executions of criminals, and compensation for losses of property came about through his efforts, which included effectively worded telegrams to Constantinople.

Now in 1911 I felt very fortunate and grateful that Reverend Ashjian was able to convince the Turkish officials at Adana to grant me a military deferment until after graduation, "since ordinary soldiers are many but educated college graduates few." I was never called again to bear arms, though four years later I was called to serve the government otherwise.

I returned to school joyously, was received with equal joy, and graduated with my class. I never had an opportunity to see St. Paul's again. Although it still exists today under American auspices, the students are Moslems or atheists. The United Church of Christ continues to finance and staff the school, even though any reference to Christianity is strictly prohibited and only secular subjects are taught. (I wonder what Col. Elliott Shepard would say about that, if he were living.) The name has been changed to Tarsus American College, and it is on a high school level.

In the summer of 1911 I was a guest lay preacher at Gaban, about twenty miles northwest of Marash. That preview convinced me that I had made the right choice for my future. In the fall of that year I returned to my birthplace and entered the Marash Theological Seminary.

8. A Theological Camelot

The Marash Theological Seminary had its roots in the Bebek Institute of Constantinople, founded in 1840 by Dr. Cyrus Hamlin. This was at first an academy, offering a general curriculum with strong emphasis on courses in religious subjects. Within a short time it evolved into two distinct schools: a four-year general course and a three-year theological graduate school. The specific mission of Bebek was to prepare Armenian clergy and other leaders to serve throughout the country. In this aim it succeeded well, as its graduates played a major role in establishing and maintaining colleges, churches, and cultural activities among all the Armenians in Turkey. In 1862 Bebek Institute was transferred to Marsovan, where it continued successfully under Armenian directors until the upheavals of the First World War. In 1863 Dr. Hamlin used the vacated Bebek Institute building to found Robert College.

My uncle Stephen, who was martyred in 1895, was a graduate of Bebek. Graduates of Bebek Institute were instrumental in starting the Marash Theological Seminary, which developed first in Aintab through the merger of two earlier schools. One was a private secondary school, flourishing since 1850 under the direction of Prof. Zenop Israelian, a Bebek alumnus. The other was an evening school started in May of 1854 by the American medical missionary, Dr. David Nutting, to train leaders for the new evangelical movement. A group of fifteen students, who worked during the day, attended informal classes in a home and studied basic academic subjects, mainly as a means of studying the Bible. These classes were conducted in Turkish, the primary language then used in Cilicia. The Bible used in the school was written in the Turkish language, transcribed with the Armenian alphabet by American missionaries. (Several generations earlier, the Cilician Armenians, by government decree, had been prohibited from using the Armenian language under penalty of having their tongues cut off. Only the Apostolic church liturgy in Classical Armenian was allowed to be recited at services. Therefore, Cilician Armenians, being more at ease with the Turkish language even in the nineteenth century, could be taught more effectively in Turkish.)

The first graduates of the new school, formed from the merger in 1855, were four of the original fifteen in Dr. Nutting's group. By 1856 Dr. Benjamin

Schneider assumed full leadership of the religious instruction in the school, and Prof. Alexan Bezjian, another Bebek graduate, of the scientific and other secular subjects, now of collegiate level. From 1855 to 1864 the school enrolled forty-two, of whom twenty-one received theological degrees. Until 1861 all the theological students were from Aintab only. Subsequently students came also from Marash, Adana, Kilis, and Antioch.

By 1865 the need for larger quarters with greater outreach was becoming obvious. Since Marash then had the largest Armenian population in Cilicia and was most easily reached from the neighboring towns (including Zeitun and about thirty others), steps were taken for relocation at Marash. Until funds could be raised for permanent buildings, temporary quarters were available in the Ak-Dereh section of the city at what eventually became the Third Armenian Evangelical Church.

This building was built under special circumstances. The Armenians of Marash had two Protestant churches in 1860, but needed a third. At that time the Turkish government would not permit the building of new churches. Only in rare instances had it allowed underground building, with the provision that the roof should be level with the street. On the other hand, Turkish law at that time did not require tearing down a building once it was completed. In order to have a new church building, a plan was devised by which the Reverend Avedis Bulghurjian, pastor of the First Church, obtained a permit to build a large residence for himself next to our home. The first floor of five rooms was completed and the second floor roughed in. He lived there for a time, then donated the building as temporary quarters for the theological seminary when it was transferred to Marash in 1865. Later, when the seminary moved to permanent quarters in 1879, this building was used for a few years as an elementary school during weekdays and for church services on Sundays. Eventually, in 1894, the second story was completed, again by special strategy. In order to minimize the noise of construction and avoid attracting attention, the floor boards were secured by screws, not nails; and to cover the noise of hammering wall boards, this work was done when the children were playing noisily in the courtyard. (It was onto the roof of this church school that my brother Luther took me to escape the Turkish soldiers when they broke into our home and killed my brothers Dicran and Samuel during the Massacre of 1895.)

As soon as the seminary began in its temporary quarters in Marash, Armenian and American clergy and laymen made a concerted effort to raise funds for a permanent campus. The Armenian Evangelical churches of Marash worked together with faculty members Dr. Christie and Reverend Montgomery locally, and with Prof. Tillman Trowbridge who went to America to raise funds. They also submitted requests to the Congregational Board for Foreign Missions for aid, while Dr. Hamlin contributed from his sums for higher education projects for Armenians in Turkey. Rev. Avedis Bulghurjian and Rev. Dicran Yenovkian were the church pastors, and Messrs. Topalian, Mouradian, and Krikor and Avedis

Jernazian (my father and uncle) were among the church council leaders in these efforts. The 650 gold pieces ($3,250) which the local Armenians donated represented great sacrifices.

The permanent campus of the Marash Theological Seminary was in the northeastern part of the city — a cluster of gleaming stone buildings separated into three sections by garden walls. In the center section were the three buildings of the seminary itself, flanked on the west by the Marash College for Girls and on the east by the two buildings of the Missionary Headquarters of the American Board.

In the warm months, this whole campus shone like a diamond amidst the emerald, ruby, and sapphire tones of the landscape. Its gardens were adorned by mulberry, walnut, and weeping willow trees as well as roses, carnations, and a host of wild flowers. An expanse of vineyards and orchards of pears, almonds, and apricots extended beyond the buildings a mile to the north, to the Taurus foothills. In winter the sparkle of the buildings was enhanced by the glitter of abundant snow. This campus inspired us.

In 1865 the curriculum of the school was comparable to the high school and junior college level, with particular stress on the study of the Bible and preaching techniques. Gradual upgrading brought the school to full collegiate status. Eventually, when colleges were established in Aintab (1874) and Tarsus (1888), the seminary curriculum was restricted to graduate courses in theology, comparable to the curricula in the American theological seminaries.

In 1895 the Turks burned the main seminary building and killed two students. The American government received indemnity from the Turkish government and rebuilt the structure. The Massacre of 1895 aroused the conscience of the world. Among the various diplomatic reactions was the threat of Russian occupation of Armenia as a gesture of protection against future persecution. England and France then convinced Turkey to relax its persecution to avoid Russian expansion. For a few years the college enjoyed a relatively peaceful existence. It served the whole Cilician population and trained leaders for cultural and religious activities. Students included women and members of the Armenian Apostolic as well as Evangelical faiths. Theological students received practical training as they assisted local and neighboring churches in various capacities. During summers, students preached in towns surrounding Marash. I spent one summer each at Goksun (about 50 miles northwest of Marash), Gaban (about 20 miles northwest of Marash), and Kilis, the town 100 miles south of Marash from which my father had brought olive trees.

During my seminary years I boarded once again at the Ebenezer Orphanage, where I again taught evening classes to boys who were trade apprentices during the day. Also I conducted evening vespers for the boys. For these services I received eight dollars a month spending money in addition to my board and room.

Graduates of Marash Theological Seminary served their communities and nation admirably as teachers or clergy. During the massacres of 1895,

1909, 1915, and 1920, they suffered with their people, and many were martyred. They gave courage and inspiration to their people to the very end. Many performed heroic deeds, showing great valor and faith. Survivors carried on as dedicated community leaders during the difficult years of reclamation and emigration. A few lived to serve parishes in countries throughout the world where Armenians migrated for survival.

With the graduation of the class of 1914 — our class — the doors of Marash Theological Seminary closed forever, and that fine institution, after fifty years of service, entered the vaults of history. There were nine of us in that class. Sarkis Chobanian, Kevork Sahagian, and Simon Vehabedian were killed very shortly after starting pastorates. Asadoor Solakian died in 1923 from a breakdown resulting from experiences in the massacres. Three survived tribulations and served their communities for many years, passing to their eternal rest within the last ten years: Nerses Sarian in 1964, and Dicran Antreasian and Harutiun Nokhutian in 1966. Only two of us remain alive, both living today (1968) in Los Angeles, California: Siragan Agbabian and myself.

As a result of the massacres, theological seminaries at Harput and Marsovan were also obliterated. In 1922, the School of Religion was started at Constantinople to carry on the work of these three seminaries. In 1925, under the Kemalist Turkish Republic, this school was banished and forced to move to Athens, Greece. In 1932, the school was combined with the Presbyterian Theological Seminary at Beirut, Lebanon, where it operates to this day as The Near East School of Theology. It receives substantial support from Armenian sources such as the Armenian Missionary Association of America.

CILICIA

When the doors of hope are opened wide,
And winter departs from our land —
Our beautiful land of Armenia,
When its balmy days shimmer and shine,
When the swallow returns to its nest,
When all the trees put on their leaves,
I long to see my Cilicia —
The world that gave me life.

  I have seen the plains of Syria,
  The mountains of Lebanon and its cedars;
  I have seen the land of Italy,
  Venice and its gondolas.
  There's no island like our Cyprus,
  And truly no place is
  As beautiful as my Cilicia —
  The world that gave me life.

    There is an age in our lives
    When all desires cease —
    An age when the spirit yearning
    Longs for its remembrances.
    When my harp grows cold
    Giving its last salute to love,
    May I repose in my Cilicia —
    The World that gave me life.

      Nahabed Roosinian

Part II
Urfa before the Battle

9. The Eye of Mesopotamia

A lmost five years had passed since my decision to prepare to fill a vacancy created by the massacre of the Armenian clergy in Adana in 1909. The time to fulfill that goal had arrived. During the last week of June in 1914, the annual convention of the Cilician Armenian Evangelical Union was held at Aintab. At this conference we graduates of the Marash Theological Seminary were examined and accepted into the ranks of professional clergy. Among the delegates was Mr. Vasil Besos of the Assyrian Protestant Church of Urfa. He was looking for a new minister for their church. He met and observed me, and felt certain that I could fill the vacancy to our mutual advantage. He urged me to accept the invitation to serve their church. Mr. Besos was a devout believer. His uncle, Reverend Jurji Shemmas (son of the founder and first pastor of the church), had served from 1902 until his martyrdom in 1909. The church had been without a pastor for the last five years. (Assyrians and Armenians in Urfa had close relationships. It was not unusual to work together). I could not refuse this call.

But I agreed to serve initially for only one year, since I had set myself a new goal which required other plans. In every community, I had observed that the medical needs of the people were as great as the spiritual needs. There was a shortage of doctors as well as clergy. Medical missionaries, who combined both services, were the most effective of all public servants. I, therefore, wanted to become a physician and a pastor. Medical training was not available in Urfa. I would have to go to Beirut where I could attend the American University of Beirut and at the same carry on pastoral work. As it turned out, God had still other plans for me. He gave me ample opportunity to serve my people, though not in medicine. I stayed in Urfa almost seven years.

Urfa is another key city in the long history of Asia Minor. It is located between the Tigris and Euphrates rivers at the juncture of ancient Syria, Armenia, and Mesopotamia, about twenty miles north of the biblical city of Harran, where Abraham lived. Wedged against the foothills of the Anatolian massif, Urfa is bounded on the north and west by barren, brown hills, while to the south and east it faces the fertile riparian plains of Mesopotamia. It is generously supplied with water by a river which comes from the northwest, encircles the northern and eastern sides of the city, and then goes down to the Euphrates. The river has had various names: Syriac Daisan or Greek Scirtos (both meaning "Leaping River"), and later Turkish Kara Kuyun (Black Well). A stream branches from the river and encircles the city along the west and south sides, although the western portion is today underground.

In the southwestern section of the city a limestone mount dominates the landscape. On the crest of the mount stands a third century Roman citadel with two slender Corinthian columns still preserved. The mount is called Nimrud's Throne. At its base are two beautiful pools. The one just north of the mount is called Zulha's Pool, a name variously ascribed to Nimrud's mother, Potiphar's wife, or Seleucus. The other lake, about one hundred feet north of this one, is called Abraham's Pool. It is named after the Hebrew patriarch because of various legends that associate him with the origin of the pools.

In one version Abraham, while passing through Urhai (Urfa), was ordered to worship pagan gods. When he refused, the Babylonian King Nimrud tried to offer him as burnt sacrifice to the gods. Abraham prayed for deliverance and was saved by Jehovah. Where he knelt, the fire was replaced by two beautiful pools, one at each knee. In Abraham's Pool are numerous carp, which have been considered sacred since ancient times and even today are fed but not eaten.

The origins of the city, dating probably from Babylonian times, are shrouded in legend. According to one popular version, it was founded by King Nimrud, son of Bel — probably the same tyrant that appears in the legend of Haik, the founder of Armenia. Early in the second millennium BC the region was infiltrated by Hurrians, Amorites, and Hittites, some of whom are considered Proto-Armenians. Subsequently under Assyrian rule the city became a thriving political and cultural center. Situated as it was at the crossroads of ancient highways running both north-south and east-west, it remained for centuries a landmark on major commercial and military routes.

The earliest name by which the site was known was Urhai or Orhay, as it appears in Syriac writings. Following its conquest by Alexander the Great, Urhai passed under Seleucid rule, was fortified and renamed Edessa by the Macedonians, after their ancient capital. During this Greek period the city achieved such renown that it was called the "Eye of Mesopotamia," and from then on, its history was well documented with written records.

In the second century BC, after the Parthian conquest that overthrew the Seleucids, Edessa became the capital of an independent principality called Osroene. It continued as a monarchy for 375 years, though at times under Roman suzerainty. All its kings took the name of Abgar. According to some scholars, several of these kings were Armenians. When Dicran the Great expanded the boundaries of Armenia in the first century BC, many Armenians migrated to Edessa. The city is noted for being the earliest seat of Syriac Christianity. The large Jewish population helped spread the new religion. In any case, Christians were allowed relative freedom in Edessa in the early years, and many Armenians as well as other peoples found refuge there from persecutions elsewhere. The legend of Abgar V's correspondence with Christ and miraculous healing is well known throughout Christendom. At the end of the fourth century AD, in preparation for the invention of the Armenian alphabet, Mesrob spent much time at the world–famous school of theology in Edessa, where Armenian scholars were prominent.

From the second century BC to the eleventh century AD Edessa found itself in the center of the struggles between eastern and western powers: between Parthia and Rome, Persia and Rome, the Arabs and Egyptians, the Arabs and Byzantium, and finally between Seljuk Moslems and Crusader Christians. Under Arab rule between the seventh and tenth centuries the city was called el-Ruha. When Byzantium recovered it in AD 1034, the name Edessa was used again. During the next century Armenians played a prominent role in the life of the city and held high positions in government. Several governors were Armenian.

When the Crusaders arrived, Armenians — including the governor Toros — gave much help to Baldwin of Boulogne. At the end of the First Crusade in 1098, a Frankish countship was established in Edessa. Its history was turbulent, however, and ended in 1144 when it was captured by a tribe of Turks. A history of this region from AD 952 to 1136 was written by the Armenian historian Matthew of Edessa, who was himself killed in the battle of 1144. The Armenian Catholicos Nerses Shnorhali wrote a deeply moving elegy on the fall of Edessa on this occasion.

After the failure of the Second Crusade to recapture the city, Edessa — once more el-Ruha — remained in various Moslem hands, never to regain its old magnificence. In the thirteenth century during Tartar and Mongol raids many Christians were killed or deported. When Tamerlane passed through in the fifteenth century, the city had been partially repopulated by Moslems. Eventually in 1637 Murad IV brought it under the Ottoman Empire. The present name of Urfa dates from this time. During a relatively peaceful interlude that followed, Armenians again came to Urfa to escape continued persecutions in other occupied districts such as Van, Sassoon, and Malatia.

By the nineteenth century Armenians constituted the largest minority in Urfa. They tried to restore the old vitality of the city — to revive its educational, literary, and other scholarly activities, rebuild its economy, and improve the living standards. But heavy taxes and other pressures on Christians made progress difficult. The Massacre of 1895 gave the Armenians of Urfa a severe blow. Six thousand were killed, three thousand being burned in the great Apostolic church. All the Armenian homes were plundered. Many were exiled. Undaunted, survivors began to rebuild. Here, as in other plundered cities in Turkey at that time, missionary aid proved most timely.

Among those who served ably during this period was Miss Corrine Shattuck, an American who had arrived in Urfa in 1892. She had endeared herself to all the Armenians and Assyrians. She had earned the respect even of the Turkish officials who called her Urfanun Meleyi (Angel of Urfa). Ibrahim Pasha, a tyrannical Kurdish feudal chief of the region called Veran Shehir, near Urfa, of whom Sultan Hamid himself was said to stand in awe, was so moved by Miss Shattuck's magnanimous spirit that he often visited her with gifts and protected the Armenians in his territory, covering a radius of about fifty miles. She proved to be a real salvation both during the massacres and in the aftermath. During the attack on December 28, 1895, she sheltered more than three hundred Armenians in her building, staunchly withstanding efforts of the Turkish horde to reach them. Afterwards she worked with unbelievable endurance, providing not only the physical necessities but also the intellectual, emotional, and spiritual needs of the surviving victims. She sent out appeals near and far, and help arrived promptly from various sources. First, she supplied food, clothing, furniture, and other essentials for survival. To help the needy keep their self-respect, and to provide a continuing source of income, she set up work programs. The embroidered handkerchiefs made by the widows at this time found a wide market in England and America. She established orphanages with schools and workshops, and also a home for the blind.

She extended her educational work to all the Armenian children in Urfa, working together with leaders of both the Evangelical and Apostolic groups. She organized "national" schools, placed leaders of both groups on boards of directors, and encouraged the Armenians to cooperate as Christians. In every area, she inspired the Armenians to work in unity as they helped themselves.

A story told by her cook poignantly reveals Miss Shattuck's complete empathy toward those she served. Miss Shattuck had worked to the point of exhaustion when the cook finally convinced her to rest and have some food. When the cook brought in a plate of chicken, Miss Shattuck, having just finished praying for her charges, said in a trembling voice, "While my Armenian sisters are eating morsels of wheat and water, how can I eat chicken? Please, take this to the sick and bring me the porridge."

Miss Shattuck had died in 1910, so I never met her. But from the moment I stepped into Urfa to the day that I left, her name was on every tongue. Her spirit remained forever a part of the heart of Urfa.

In 1896 Miss Effie Chambers, another American missionary, came to Urfa to help Miss Shattuck. She, too, gave devoted service. She quickly learned the language and played an important role in the Armenian educational program in Urfa. In 1905 Miss Chambers was transferred to Kessab and there, too, became a blessing for the young people there.

In 1914 when I arrived, the Armenians of Urfa were still enjoying a cultural revival. The population of the city was about 75,000: 45,000 Turks, 25,000 Armenians, 5,000 Assyrians, and a few Jews and others. Over the years, most of the Jews had emigrated. The Armenian quarter covered the western half of the city from within the old city walls at the north, along the base of Telfedur Hill, to the region of the two lakes in the south. The Assyrians were concentrated at the northeastern corner of the city. Arabs and Kurds were generally in the outlying villages. One exclusively Armenian village several miles to the northeast of the city, Garmuj, had 5,000 inhabitants. Feudalistic farms in and around Urfa produced wheat, barley, cotton, grapes, and dairy products. Rich quarries in the vicinity of Urfa furnished the stones with which almost all the buildings in the city were built. Armenians mined these quarries. When they were killed, the mining stopped, and the Turks resorted to tearing down Armenian buildings to obtain stones for new structures. Armenian builders of this district had a reputation for excellence, dating back hundreds of years. In 1087 Armenian architects from Edessa were employed to construct the three fine gates of Cairo, Egypt. Armenian artisans of Urfa produced outstanding works in wood, metals, leather, textiles, and rugs. Fine camel-bone and ivory combs made exclusively by Armenians were much in demand. Seventy-five percent of the merchants were Armenians and carried on an extensive import-export trade. Most of the professionals, especially medical personnel, were Armenian. A few government positions, especially those requiring skills and trust, were held by Armenians.

In addition to the traces of the various civilizations that remained in the city itself — such as the walls, the citadel, and columns with inscriptions, and the many Christian churches transformed into mosques — interesting and valuable historical remnants could be found in the hills outside the city. Here were numerous cave tombs with mosaics, inscriptions, statuary, and other evidences of the lifestyles of the early inhabitants of Urfa.

10. *Seferberlik*

I had been in Urfa hardly one month when on that fateful day of July 28, 1914, World War I broke out. Its shadows spread over the city and changed all our dreams into new nightmares. Urfa — situated in a key position in relation to Aleppo, Diarbakir, and Mosul — had an important role to play in the strategy for the expansion of the German empire.

Toward the end of the nineteenth century Germany had taken a pro-Turkish policy in Russo-Turkish territorial conflicts, and was sending military advisors to train Turkish soldiers. Turkey, in return, gave Germany concessions to build the Berlin to Bagdad Railway, essential to furthering the new plan of *Drang nach Osten* (Push to the East). While other European powers made attempts — sporadic and ineffectual though they might have been — to solicit reforms in the Turkish treatment of minorities (especially Armenians), Germany had been careful not to offend Turkish sensibilities. It was natural, therefore, that Turkey should sign a treaty of alliance with Germany on August 3, 1914.

One week later, on August 10, the topic of conversation everywhere was those red posters decorated with guns and sabres which had been placed by the government on walls in every town and hamlet from one end of the country to the other. These posters officially declared *seferberlik* (mobilization and martial law). No one could comprehend their full significance. Mobilization for what purpose?

Although in its foreign policy Turkey maintained its official neutrality for almost three more months, internally the country feverishly prepared for war. Assertions that an unwilling Turkey was maneuvered into the war through a series of "fateful incidents" are the usual Turkish misrepresentations of all their crimes. The final, so-called fateful incident occurred on October 29. The German ships Goeben and Breslau had escaped from a Mediterranean naval battle and entered into Turkish waters. Instead of being dismantled, as they should have been according to international law, they were permitted by the Turks to fly the Turkish flag and change their names to Jawus and Midilli. Thus, the ships became Turkish ships, though they kept their German crews and remained under the command of the German Admiral Souchon. They bombed the Russian Black Sea port of Odessa, and when Turkey did not protest against this act committed by the

Germans under cover of the Turkish flag, it became obvious that the Turks had made up their minds to join Germany in the war. Russia declared war on Turkey on November 4, Britain the next day, and France the following day.

For those of us in the interior who had witnessed activities in Turkey for months earlier, and particularly the preparations during the seferberlik — little known by the outside world — it was quite obvious that the decision for war had already been made long ago. The incident involving the German warships was a subterfuge to absolve Turkey of blame for entering the war. In fact, even the apologist historians record that on July 28, the very day that World War I started, Turkey initiated the steps which resulted within one week in the treaty of alliance with Germany, mentioned above.

Actually, the war was welcomed by Turkey as a means of ignoring an agreement it had been forced to make with the European powers following the International Conference of 1913. By February of 1914 the major powers had devised and adopted a new plan in an attempt to prevent further persecutions of Armenians in Turkey and to resolve the Armenian question. The Ottoman vizier and foreign minister had signed the accord. Turkish Armenia was to be divided into two provinces: one incorporating the southern *vilayets* (provinces) of Van, Bitlis, Harput, and Diarbakir; the other including the northern vilayets of Sivas and Erzerum and adding a seventh, Trebizond. By April, two governors under international auspices had been selected for the provinces of Turkish Armenia: the Norwegian Colonel Hoff for the vilayets around Van in the south, and the Dutch Colonel Westenenk for the vilayets around Erzerum in the north. A few weeks later, they had arrived in Constantinople for briefings. By the summer of 1914 Hoff was in Van, and Westenenk was about to leave for Erzerum. When World War I broke out, they were promptly dismissed from Turkey. The fragile hopes for reforms which would end persecution were dashed to pieces.

The militant, fanatical Ittihadists then in control of the Turkish government considered the war a heaven-sent opportunity to solve the Armenian question in their own way — that is, to annihilate the Armenian nation. The Turkish government was fearful that Armenia, like the Balkans, might eventually become independent, and had determined to stop this at any cost. The major powers, being involved in a life and death struggle, could do nothing to prevent the Genocide. In fact, Germany — who might have helped — actually promoted the plan; it preferred Armenia without Armenians to eliminate any economic roadblocks as it sought to gain control of Asia Minor.

Some German individuals and groups tried valiantly to convince the German government to use its influence to stop the Turkish excesses. Notable in these efforts was the German "Mission of the East," whose chief moving force was Dr. Johannes Lepsius. He was a veritable Isaiah battling for the salvation of the Armenian people. But all these efforts were in vain. Dr. Lepsius narrowly escaped internment in Germany, and perhaps murder, by fleeing to Holland before his travel papers were recalled. Other pro-Armenian workers in Germany were coerced by the diplomatic representatives to end a strong press campaign, which was attracting widespread attention to the massacres. The government attempted to justify this censorship on the basis that such a campaign might heighten Turkish antagonism toward Armenians and increase their persecution.

After the war, Dr. Lepsius reorganized his mission and worked with equal dedication to rehabilitate the refugees. He continued for many years to speak out on behalf of justice for the Armenians.

11. The Military Draft — Turkish Style

I was a young boy in 1895 when I first experienced the terror of massacre. In my youth in 1909 I passed through the fiery circuit a second time. But, horrible as these two ordeals were, they were merely a small spark compared to the intense conflagration of the genocide that took place between 1915 and 1922. I witnessed this barbarism as an adult, during my stay in Urfa.

At the end of 1914 the real intent of the Turkish government with respect to the Armenian population was not obvious. When Turkey entered the war in November and the sultan declared *jihad*, the fears of the Armenians were allayed as the sultan explained, "This is a jihad against the outside infidel *giavoors*, not against our own Christian subjects." The Armenians knew from past experience that the Turks always sought an opportunity to persecute Christians, but the Turkish alliance with Germany and Austria gave some hope that this relationship might inject civilized restraint into the barbarians. Unfortunately, time revealed the contrary, as my story will show. The alliance provided more clever, more diabolical methods for persecution.

Within a month after *seferberlik* was announced, universal conscription was ordered as a necessary measure under the state of war. All males between the ages of 19 and 45 were called for military service. As the war progressed, the age limit was extended to 50, then 55. The right to bear arms was a privilege that had been given the Armenians less than a decade earlier. Before the adoption of the constitution in 1908, Armenians were called *rayah* (cattle) and subjected to various types of discrimination even in relatively calm periods between massacres. One measure of discrimination was that Armenians were forbidden to bear arms and, therefore, were barred from military service. Instead, they were compelled to pay a tax called *bedel* during the three-year period when they were of the age of military service for full citizens. The Turks themselves had the option of choosing between service and bedel. (It must be pointed out that being prohibited from service in the military and being exempt from military service had completely opposite connotations, although both resulted in exclusion. Prohibition was degrading, exemption a privilege.) In 1908 the constitution supposedly granted equal status to all and gave everyone the choice between bedel and service. This change in policy received international attention. I remember a newspaper account at that time of a visit made by a group of young Armenians to President Theodore Roosevelt in the United States. They had asked his advice on the subject of military options. He had advised, "Tell your young men to sign up for military duty." This was hardly the policy among Turks. Usually those who could afford the $250 fee chose bedel. Those who could afford only a partial payment gave that as a bribe to an official who released them from service. When the war broke out, these officials amassed great fortunes in a short time. Those who could not afford payment at all often either left town before induction or escaped en route. Deserters were everywhere and many survived by robbery.

Conditions in the Turkish army at that time gave ample reason for desertion. A condemned deserter, while being raised to the gallows in Urfa, announced, "I entered service and served my sultan faithfully. I was hungry and naked in the army, and my family at home was destitute. Who can stand this? Let me tell you, if I could rise from the dead, if you were to treat me again the same way as a soldier, and if I knew that I'd be hanged, I'd still desert." He was speaking for many soldiers. There was so much graft and inefficiency in the military administration that most of the food meant for soldiers, and the funds marked for it, were appropriated by the officers, leaving the fighting man only soup that was not much more than murky hot water. Likewise, because of corruption, clothes and supplies were pitifully inadequate. Not only that, but the ordinary soldier, while worrying about his destitute family at home, had to put up with the harassment of an illiterate, stupid, and sadistic sergeant. All in all, desertion with the risk of facing capture and execution seemed to offer more chance of survival than the tortures of service.

Under the new universal conscription, Armenians were made the subject of additional discrimination. Exemptions were almost impossible for Armenians, easy for Turks. Nevertheless, Armenians became dutiful and valuable soldiers in the Turkish army. Enver Pasha, minister of war and commander-in-chief, praised the Armenians as faithful and valuable citizens, and acknowledged in the press that Armenian soldiers served more loyally and valiantly than the Turks themselves. Armenian soldiers suppressed and transcended their natural sympathy for the Allies and, even in trying physical circumstances, performed their duties well in the Turkish army. Armenian soldiers had, in fact, saved Enver Pasha's life at the Caucasus front. But what reward did the loyal Armenian soldier receive for his services? In the end, the "equal status" was short-lived, and the "right to bear arms" evolved into a death warrant for Armenian draftees.

After 1915 bedel was categorically denied to Armenians. Induction was used as a preliminary to mass murder. Shortly after Armenian soldiers were admitted into military ranks, their guns were taken away from them, and they were placed in *amala tabour* (work battalions). Then, being rendered defenseless, they were murdered en masse. The only recompense the faithful Armenian soldier received for his labors was execution by those he served. (I will describe episodes of these murders as I tell the story of the war in and around Urfa.) By 1916 the Turkish army was so depleted that the bedel option was eventually eliminated for Turks, too. Bribery still persisted, however, and provided handsome profits for Turkish officials.

12. Three Bags of Rice

I n addition to conscription, a second measure which went into effect promptly after the declaration of a state of war was the appropriation of civilian property for military use. Authorized military personnel entered stores and took food, clothing, or anything else that might be useful as "military goods" and gave as payment promissory notes redeemable in the future. That future never came. Armenian shopkeepers were almost stripped in the process, whereas Turkish shopkeepers were required to give very little. Mr. Ignatius Shemmas, a prominent Assyrian businessman, uncle of Vasil Besos who was responsible for my coming to Urfa, was the manager of a large handwork production agency. He was my neighbor and often brought me critical or interesting local news. One story he told was of an episode connected with the collection of military goods. The porter involved had gleefully told Mr. Shemmas about the incident.

An official collector of military goods appropriated three bags of rice from a store and hired a porter to move them to the armory. When the porter began to load up the bags, the officer whispered, "Take two of these bags to my home and one to the armory." The porter answered, "Very well, Sir" and began to transport the bags. When the officer went home that evening, he saw only one bag. Angrily he called the porter to him and questioned, "Where is the other bag of rice?" The porter very calmly replied, "Sir, you will forgive me if I tell you that I made a more equitable distribution. I took one bag to the armory, one to your home, and one to *my* home." All that the enraged officer could say was, "Get away and don't let me set eyes on you again!"

Opportunities for official graft and harassment of Armenians were greatest in rural areas. Officers were sent to collect wheat, barley, and cattle from outlying villages. Upon entering, they would first terrorize the Armenians with beatings, then confiscate the goods. Villagers took turns as lookouts to issue warnings of approaching officials. The farmers would then run away to avoid being tortured, even though they would still lose their property. Each village had an assigned quota of products to supply. The officers in charge of collections devised methods for collecting more and increasing their own wealth. This typical episode illustrates one technique.

In a town whose quota might be 100 sheep, the collector demands 200, then magnanimously sells back 100 of the poorest animals for one *mejid* apiece. He keeps the money. On the way back to town, by prior arrangement a confederate meets the collector at a designated place, bringing the skins of ten dead sheep. These are exchanged for ten of the best, live animals, which the confederate takes away to sell. Back in town at government headquarters the collector delivers ninety sheep and ten skins, saying that these ten died on the way into town and soliloquizing on the great difficulties encountered in the assignment. His word is not questioned, since the chief at headquarters knows he, too, will receive a share of the profits from the sale of the ten stolen animals. The collector expresses his willingness to repeat the task in spite of the hardships, and his assignment is renewed.

Still another method of extortion involved housing for officers who were stationed in Urfa. About ten or twelve private homes were needed for this purpose. The government selected about one hundred Armenian homes, and took ten to fifteen lira from each who wanted to be exempt from this obligation.

The appropriation of civilian property for military use continued in this manner for the duration of the war. One result was that in 1917-18 a terrible famine struck throughout the country and thousands of poverty-stricken people died.

13. Restraint

The Armenians in Urfa resigned themselves to the increased harassment brought on by martial law, conscription, and the appropriation of property. They had managed to live with discrimination in normal times and could survive these harsher measures in wartime. Everyone expected this war to be a short one, and many hoped that the peace afterwards would still bring the long-awaited reforms. In fact, they made every effort to cooperate with the Turks in the extra demands, in order to stay on good terms and to pave the way for working out the goals of the Constitution of 1908 after the war. Little by little, however, distressing and then alarming measures were imposed. From the spring of 1915 to the end of September, over a period of about five months, the Armenians gradually were forced to realize that cooperation and appeasement had brought them to the point of complete annihilation, worse than any of the previous massacres. In the end, they put up a valiant defense and died a heroic death, with very few surviving.

The first warning came early in the spring of 1915. One day we found the Armenian gendarmes in the city very dejected. They told us that their guns had been taken away from them and that they were being sent to Aleppo. The news was ominous, and we did not have to wait long for its sequel. On April 5, the whole Armenian quarter was suddenly blockaded, and Turkish police and gendarmes began searching Armenian homes one by one. (Police were civilians. Gendarmes were military police. By this time no Armenian gendarmes were left. As for the police, Armenians were not admitted to their ranks.) Silent dread settled over the whole quarter. What was the government looking for, and why? No explanation was given. A few bags of documents and a handful of guns were collected. Several persons were arrested and jailed on imaginary charges: "Nazar is going to make guns for the Russians when they come." "Boghos wants the enemy to come to Urfa so he can make money by selling them wheat." These searches and arrests then continued sporadically. At first the Turkish police and gendarmes worked in an orderly fashion. As time went on, they began robbing and raping and generally vandalizing the Armenian quarter.

The climax to this first series of arrests came on May 27, when twenty Armenian community leaders were seized. The next day my good friend

Mr. Shemmas approached me with an important piece of news: "Hakku Effendi sent me to tell you that very shortly two gendarmes will come to invite you to the office of the *mutesarif pasha* [title given to the head of a *sanjak* or district] to translate the Armenian, French, and English writings seized from the Armenian homes." Hakku Effendi was an Assyrian clerk in the local government offices and knew what was going on. Since no Turk in town knew the required four languages, the officials had asked the American missionaries for the names of Assyrians who could do the job. The missionaries could name only two persons: Ibrahim Fawzil, a graduate of Aintab College, and Effrayim Jernazian, graduate of St. Paul's College and Marash Theological Seminary. Since I was pastor of an Assyrian church, it appears that my being Armenian was overlooked.

Hardly had Mr. Shemmas finished his words when the officers arrived with the invitation. At the district offices, the Mutesarif Ali Haydar and other officials most politely explained to me that they needed my services as interpreter. Mr. Fawzil, a member of my congregation, who was very sympathetic toward Armenians, was designated as my assistant. Of course, it was impossible to refuse, although the risks were obvious. At any rate, here was an unexpected opportunity to serve my people. The fate of many depended on the interpretation of those manuscripts. I said a silent prayer as I accepted: "Your Honor, I shall serve in any way I can."

After my identification papers were approved, I was led to a meeting hall where, around a large table, were seated members of the Divani Harp (Military Tribunal), charged with the disposition of the confiscated papers. The *reisi* (chairman) was Ismael Bey, the local director of education. His assistant was Shakir Bey, police captain, son-in-law of Mahmoud Nedim, an influential parliamentary representative. One additional member of the committee was a local official. Two others were from Constantinople. The committee members, like those who spoke to me earlier, were not at all concerned about my being Armenian. They, too, were very courteous, and we started work immediately.

At one end of the hall were rows of cloth and leather bags filled with manuscripts, notebooks, and books brought from Armenian homes. They placed the bags before me one by one, to read their contents and translate into Turkish. Ibrahim Fawzil was also present. He and I were the only ones in the room who knew English. From the beginning we communicated with each other in English concerning what we should say and do. No one objected.

This flagrant indifference to security measures seems amazing and unbelievable to people who hear these stories today. How could these officials accept an Armenian for this job and allow private communication in English during the proceedings? How could they give me access to all the communications at government headquarters? At that time such apparent negligence was not so astonishing. It was just part of governmental inefficiency. We simply considered ourselves lucky whenever official carelessness worked in our favor. Furthermore, in retrospect it would appear that the local officials had not yet reached a highly fanatical dedication to the Genocide and were more interested in finding new sources of extortion. As for the really fanatical Ittihadist officials from Constantinople, among whom was the Mutesarif Ali Haydar, they perhaps were not very serious about the early procedures either, since they knew they were going to kill us all eventually anyway.

Though the committee appeared courteous and lenient in some ways, we could not be sure what might trigger a change in attitude. They were not willing to let any papers slip by, and demanded a full translation of each item. (Usually an oral translation was enough, but sometimes they asked us to put it in writing.) Ibrahim Fawzil and I, therefore, had to maintain a calm cautious approach. We had to satisfy the committee with our work and at the same time try to prevent the arrest of our people.

The first day of translation was very trying and seemed more like a year to me. That same evening I called together Reverend Ardavazt Kalendarian, Prelate of the Armenian Apostolic Church, Reverend Solomon Akkelian, Pastor of the Armenian Evangelical Church, and a group of young men from each church. I begged them to tell everyone to hide or burn any guns, letters, manuscripts, books, or pictures that might in any way be construed as "revolutionary." At the end of the meeting Reverend Kalendarian pressed my hand: *"Badveli* [Reverend], my brother, your being called as interpreter is a miracle of Providence. Carry on, and rest assured, the Lord will guide you. He wants you to serve your nation in this way."

One of my first actions upon arrival at Urfa had been to establish working relations with the other clergy of the city as well as with the lay leaders. Among them I had found Reverend Kalendarian very cooperative. We always consulted about community affairs and exchanged significant pieces of information. Under the *millet* (nation) system of government, we represented our respective religious communities on the Mejlisi Idareh (City Council). In the Ottoman Empire, as in many European countries, church and state were not separated but integrated. The head of the secular government was also the religious head of the people. Accordingly, the civil affairs of each millet or religio-ethnic group were administered by the head of its church. This administrator represented his group on the town council. In Urfa the deputy for the Apostolic community was Reverend Kalendarian, while I represented the Protestant community (including all ethnic groups). Before each council meeting we met to discuss matters so that we would be prepared to take a common stand on issues critical to the Armenian community in those uneasy times.

Daily confiscations continued. The mound of letters and books increased. While performing my duties as interpreter, from my vantage point at the government offices, I heard many of the daily reports from central Turkish headquarters in Constantinople. Security measures continued to be very lax. No effort was made to prevent me from overhearing anything that went on. The directives from the party chiefs of the Ittihad ve Terakki regime clearly revealed a firm determination to eliminate the Armenians, who constituted one large segment of the non-Turkish people in the country.

Each evening I tried to pass on critical information to those who would be affected. I was not always successful in convincing the people I tried to warn. I was unable to convince most of the other Armenian religious and political leaders that the local Turks, with whom they had had reasonably smooth relations for at least five years, could be capable of treachery. For me, a relative newcomer who had direct knowledge of Turkish orders from headquarters, the facts were not only believable, they were obvious and alarming, and called for quick, defensive action. For them, my viewpoint seemed unreliable and dangerous, since I was new and, they emphasized, unfamiliar with life in Urfa in recent years. Some even felt a little uneasy, considering my views inconsistent with my role as clergyman.

Such a one at first was the young and kindly American missionary, Mr. Francis H. Leslie, although he later revised his opinions. I knew him from my student days at the theological seminary where he had lectured to us for a time. In Urfa he held the position formerly filled by Miss Shattuck and Miss Chambers. Mr. Leslie was dedicated in his educational and humanitarian work on behalf of the Armenians, but the political difficulties he had to face eventually proved more than he could handle. His problems started early. Shortly after the war began, about five hundred interned foreigners — English, French, and Russian — were transported to Urfa from various other towns in Turkey. They were not persecuted and were permitted to move about freely. Their respective governments sent each a specific sum of money for personal needs. Those sums came monthly to Mr. Leslie for distribution, as he was a representative of a non-belligerent country. Turkish officials started harassing him to appropriate some of the money for themselves. He informed Jesse Jackson, the American Consul at Aleppo who, to strengthen Mr. Leslie's position, made the necessary arrangements to have him appointed vice-consul. An American flag was placed on Mr. Leslie's headquarters. The Turks paid no attention to this. They tore down the flag, got hold of the money designated for the evacuees, and distributed it as they pleased. Even after this experience, Mr. Leslie still believed that the Armenians should accept, without protest, all demands made on them by the Turks.

One who did believe in active resistance toward oppression was Mgrdich Yotneghparian, a dynamic and fearless young man who eventually led the Armenian Battle of Defense in Urfa. He was the great-grandson of the patriarch Garabed Yotneghparian who had established the family in Urfa in the late eighteenth century. In 1915 the descendants numbered about two hundred families. Born in 1882, Mgrdich was the fourth of six sons. He had one sister four years younger. While his older brothers Kevork (b.1875), Nerses (b.1877), and Hovannes (b.1880) carried on the family business as farriers and maintained supportive establishments such as a caravanserai and water mill, Mgrdich was too restless to study or to work. But even as a young boy he showed qualities of leadership — determination, great ingenuity and daring, and skill in rallying his playmates to do his bidding. He organized the Armenian boys into groups and encouraged fights as training for self defense against gangs of Turkish boys who frequently attacked them. When the Yotneghparian parents died in 1893 and 1894, Kevork (thirteen years older) kept a watchful eye on Mgrdich. The brother Nerses went out on business trips among the nomadic Kurdish and Arab tribesmen. Kevork sent Mgrdich on these trips, not because Nerses needed help but to give the younger boy an outlet for his energy. Mgrdich happily fraternized with the nomads and from them learned to ride and hunt. He learned the Kurdish and Arabic languages so well that he could even use various dialects like the natives. He also became very familiar with the regions extending considerably beyond Urfa, as far as Diarbakir and Aleppo. All these skills and knowledge later proved most useful as he frequently used disguises to perform his deeds. Joining Mgrdich in his operations was his younger brother Sarkis. Born in 1893, the year his father died, he had lost the sight of one eye through illness. He became such an excellent marksman that he was nicknamed Asdoo Peepuh (God's Eyeball).

The Massacre of 1895 left an indelible mark on Mgrdich, then thirteen years old. He was twenty-six when in 1908 the Young Turks proclaimed the new era of democracy and equality. While other young Armenians responded optimistically to these pronouncements, Mgrdich remained very skeptical. His suspicions were reinforced by the Cilician massacre the following year. Throughout the period of the Balkan wars he laid plans for what he considered the inevitable battle for Armenian survival, and gathered weapons and supplies for that fight. In 1915 Mgrdich and his followers sensed that the Turkish government was not to be trusted and that if massacres should begin as in the past, no help could come from outside sources. As soon as the first signs of new persecution appeared, this group urged their fellow Armenians to prepare for defense. Repeatedly, as official provocations arose in increasing severity, Mgrdich tried to lead an armed protest. Repeatedly he was restrained by the Armenian clergy and political leaders.

14. Warning from Zeitun

The first opportunity of the Armenians in Urfa to stage an armed defense against increasing harassment presented itself in June of 1915. Throughout the early spring of that year the Turks had been in a general state of dejection. The military reverses suffered at the hands of the Allies both in the Caucasus in December and at the Suez Canal in February had given them cause for worry. But by the end of May we noticed smiles on their faces. We wondered what victory they had achieved. We soon found out. The Turks had finally succeeded in driving the Armenians out of Zeitun.

In previous years on many occasions the Armenians of Zeitun had been under Turkish attack. They had fought courageously and resisted several weeks each time until exhaustion and European intervention had ended the siege, permitting the people of the city to resume life as usual. I had seen such an incident during my year at Zeitun.

This time the pattern changed. The Turks did not attack directly but resorted to treachery. They coerced several leaders of the Armenian community in Marash to join a delegation of Turkish officials to Zeitun. Their mission was to persuade the Armenians of Zeitun that they would enjoy peace and security if they would, firstly, give up their guns to the government and secondly, migrate to a new region several miles away. The Protestant minister (Rev. Aharon Shirajian) and the Apostolic priest (Rev. Sahag Der Bedrosian) were among the delegation forced to come from Marash. The director of the trade school at the German orphanage, Herr Blank, accompanied them. The clergymen and other delegates from Marash had been threatened with dire consquences to themselves and to Zeitun if they refused. They had no choice. Neither did the people of Zeitun. Most of the young fighters had been drafted. Refusal to turn over guns or to leave the city meant instant annihilation. This time a fully activated Turkish army with powerful weapons, including German Mausers, was at hand to see to that. The Allies were certainly in no position to intervene. Both the visiting Armenians from Marash and the local Armenian leaders in Zeitun reasoned that exodus might mean survival for some. Thus, the caravans started out warily but hopefully. The few able-bodied men who had not been taken into the army were placed in a separate caravan and sent away, some toward Konia and some to Bagdad. Very few of them survived the ordeals they experienced. The rest of the population — including women, children, and a few old men — were directed towards Urfa.

The young men of Zeitun who had been conscripted into the Turkish army had been placed in work battalions. Some of them appeared in Urfa among a group of about 1,200 Armenian soldiers brought in late spring to build a road. These soldiers included natives of Marash, Aintab, Gaban, and other Cilician towns as well as Zeitun. Their guns had been confiscated and replaced with shovels and picks. The first week at Urfa they were given liberty to move about the city at will. Some of them were friends of mine from school and orphanage. One morning I invited about twenty-five of them to my home and listened to their stories. They told of the destruction of their towns and begged me, "Tell the Armenians of Urfa to prepare to defend themselves right now. We are ready to fight and die with them. Giving in to Turkish demands will not guarantee their safety. Let them not be fooled like us. We should have stayed in our towns and fought to defend them. At least we would have died honorably." These men had gone into the army believing they had been conscripted to participate in the war. Now they realized that they had been conscripted just to be removed from their towns so their homes would be defenseless.

That night I met with the Prelate Ardavazt, several church leaders, some political leaders, and Mgrdich to give the message of the soldiers. The prelate and the church elders believed that appeasement would be wiser in Urfa. After all, they reasoned, cities like Zeitun had a record of numerous "revolts." Urfa had been law-abiding. Armenian political leaders in Urfa did, however, have a history of favoring preparations for defense. After the massacre of 1909 in Adana, suspecting that similar incidents might occur again in the future, they had begun a plan of defense. Nevertheless, in the spring of 1915 they had no intention of putting this plan into operation. Most of them felt that they should resort to armed resistance only out of desperation if all else failed. Even though the situation was becoming steadily worse in Urfa, they felt the solution still was not in using guns because that would give the government a pretext for all-out persecution. On the other hand, local Turkish officials might be willing to come to reasonable terms if Armenians would continue to show their loyalty and give certain sums of money in payment for guarantees of security.

Mgrdich Yotneghparian sensed that the Turkish decision to crush the Armenians was final and would spare no town, and that negotiations would be futile. The only means of self-preservation was to fight immediately. Waiting would do nothing but reduce the numbers and strength of the Armenians. He could not bear the soft approach. He left the meeting in utter frustration but with greater determination than ever to pursue his guerrilla activities and to prepare for eventual, total armed resistance. "I will never let the people of Urfa be driven into exile! I will go into hiding and do what I must. As for you, all of you will, without a doubt, head toward a slaughter, in spite of all the tribute you may pay to save yourselves."

Three Armenian soldiers from the work battalion returned to me the next day, as arranged, to learn what the townspeople had decided. Disappointed and dejected, they returned to their quarters. Armenian and Assyrian soldiers from Urfa were soon added to their ranks. The battalion was divided into two sections. One was sent to work at Kudemma just outside the city and on the road leading to the desert of Der-el-Zor, and the other to Kara Koepru (Black Bridge), a few miles in the opposite direction, toward Diarbakir.

One day during that same month of June, while the Armenian soldiers at Kudemma were working on the road, they saw a group of tired and worn women and children passing by. Soldiers and deportees recognized each other. The deportees were the families of many of the laborers — mothers, sisters, wives, children — in shattered condition, being driven toward the wilderness. These were part of the exiles from Zeitun, pitiful remnants of the "pilgrim" caravans who had been promised greater "peace and security" as they were led out of their homes toward new regions "a short distance away." Hardly out of their city, they had been attacked by Turkish soldiers and ruffians, robbed, raped, beaten, and killed as they were driven on. When they saw the Armenian soldiers, their apathy was replaced by agitation. Sounds of weeping and wailing filled the air. Children moaned, "Daddy, take us home again!" These soldiers and deportees tried to rush toward each other for at least one last embrace. Even that was not to be allowed! Turkish soldiers and gendarmes kept the families apart with their whips and bayonets. Husbands, sons, and brothers silently bore their burden as they labored on. Miserable and mournful, the mothers, wives, sisters, and children struggled along, continuing their road to Golgotha.

At Urfa the exiles were interned for a two-day "rest" in the Jerid Square section of town. Military guards were placed around them, supposedly for protection. Actually, the soldiers prevented the refugees from going to the market for food, and obstructed the efforts of the local townspeople to help the refugees. These gendarmes who were escorting the exiles bore themselves as proudly as if they had vanquished the British army. After Urfa, the exiles from Zeitun — like their compatriots from many other towns — were driven into the desert of Der-el-Zor from which few, if any, survived.

We Armenians in the Ottoman Empire had been accustomed to episodes of persecution with imprisonment and slaughter, but this system of torture and mass annihilation through exile and forced marches was a new phenomenon which we could not even have imagined. In the weeks following the appearance of the first refugees from Zeitun, Urfa was to become very familiar with the new technique, as refugees filed in from many parts of Armenia. The Armenians in Urfa still could not believe that this calamity could come to their city, too.

15. Three Taps of the Pen

O ne day toward the end of my first week at court, even as the Armenian leaders were hoping to avoid an armed protest and to gain security through peaceful negotiations with the local Turks, I learned from the tribunal that the second mass arrest of Armenians was scheduled for the next day. These would be primarily political leaders. Their papers would be seized also. I went that evening to warn Mr. Antranig Ferid (Bozajian), head of the *Dashnagtsutiune* (one of the Armenian political parties) and superintendent of the Armenian Apostolic Schools of Urfa, and suggested that he warn others and leave town or hide. He refused to believe that he was in any danger. He thought that the Ittihadists were still his friends, and that they would release him. He allowed himself to be imprisoned.

The morning after his arrest, when I entered the court, Shakir Bey placed a sack before me. He pulled out a large notebook and handed it to me saying, "My boy, I want you to examine this notebook and translate it for me." When I opened it and saw the contents, a cold sweat covered my forehead. The sack of papers belonged to Mr. Antranig. The notebook placed before me contained everything the Turkish government wanted!

It was the membership list of the Dashnagtsutiune and the outline of the Armenian plan of defense drawn up in the aftermath of the massacre of 1909. It included names and posts of the participants (Gaidzag, Shant, Raffi, and Trootsig groups). To explain away such a document would have been impossible. Translating that notebook meant opening the door to a myriad of horrors.

I suggested to Shakir Bey, "Sir, these are lists of names — like a professor's rollbook. It would be more valuable if I would translate other letters and documents." To my great relief, he agreed to postpone the translation of the notebook. Ramzi Bey, however, a member of the tribunal from Constantinople, wanted to know the names. He was suspicious and suggested that the owner of the list be brought into court for an explanation.

Mr. Antranig was brought from his cell. When he entered the courtroom, he was buoyant and self-assured. When confronted with the list, he explained brightly, "When you took over the government a few years ago, you told us to keep our Dashnag organization active so that in case the sultan's forces try to stir up trouble, we would be ready to help you put them down. So, this is our roster." Ramzi Bey sneered, "*Biz dedik. Siz deh inandunuz. Ahmahk millet.* [We said it, and you believed it. Stupid nation.]", Ramzi Bey would have continued to cross-examine and taunt Mr. Antranig, but the chairman, Ismael Bey, seemed uncomfortable and eager to stop the probing. He ordered the prisoner to be returned to his cell, the translation of his notebook postponed, and the next set of papers brought out. I suspect he was afraid that Antranig's papers might reveal embarrassing facts about the local Ittihadists and preferred not to take a chance that these might be exposed. Also, the local men on the tribunal, with their very sharp instinct for recognizing opportunities for bribery, may have understood more from my reluctance to translate than I realized. The possibility that they were open to bribery gradually dawned on me as the day wore on.

That evening I went to the diocesan headquarters of the Apostolic Church again and described the new predicament. The prelate and those around him agreed that desperate measures would have to be taken. I suggested two alternatives: if possible, to arrange that night to buy the notebook from Shakir Bey, or, if that were impossible, to set fire that night to the hall where those notebooks were kept. Without delay the prelate called an emergency meeting of all the elders of the congregation and presented the problem to them. After much serious deliberation, it was decided to offer Ismael Bey and Shakir Bey a sum of money to purchase the notebook, to remove it from among the papers of Antranig Ferid. Khosrof Dadian, city treasurer, and Giragos Shamlian were sent to consult with them immediately.

Late that night I received word that the arrangements to purchase the notebook had been accepted. I had devised a signal. Whichever notebook I tapped three times with my pen during the court session would be the one to be removed from Antranig's sack. I was pleased with my success so far, but I was by no means certain of the final outcome. Perhaps, as soon as I gave the signal, the committee would arrest me as a traitor and hang me. In the morning before I left home, I said my prayers, wrote my last will and testament, and calling two of my neighbors, revealed the situation to them. With tearful eyes they gave me encouragement and prayerfully sent me on my way.

When I entered the committee room, Ismael Bey and Shakir Bey were more cordial than usual. We started work at once. After we had reviewed several other letters and notebooks, Shakir Bey handed me Antranig's notebook. My heart started to pound, but without showing my emotion I took the notebook and, making some explanatory remarks, I drummed the notebook idly with my pen three times. At the third tap I was expecting to be seized, removed to the inner torture room, and killed. I knew this was the usual procedure for those declared enemies. I breathed with genuine relief when Shakir Bey smiled and said, "Very well, Vaiz [Preacher] Effendi, let me have that notebook, and you go ahead with the other papers."

I again went home alive. My compatriots had been spared torture and execution, at least for a while. That evening I told the prelate the good news.

Together we prayed and thanked God for this deliverance. Ismael Bey had kept his word and relinquished the notebook. It was burned that night. Ferid was spared instant execution. He and three teachers arrested with him were sent to Aleppo for further interrogations and trial.

Antranig's notebook was probably the most dangerous item to pass before me during the months of work in the government office. Still, every day documents appeared which might be interpreted in such a way as to furnish cause for arrest. If, on the other hand, I were to be found concealing any papers, or if I should refuse to translate any, torture and death could be my lot. I was alarmed at either prospect, so had to find a solution. I devised a plan which, though it involved some risk of being discovered, avoided both dangers. Each day, as I handled the stacks of papers, I was able unobtrusively to set aside those that appeared potentially incriminating. There were enough other papers to keep us steadily occupied, so none on the committee questioned my procedures. After the officials departed for the day, I used to order the policeman assigned to help me and Mr. Fawzil to sell those "excess papers" to the local public bath for use as fuel. The policeman kept the money or tobacco received in payment, and without once suspecting my motives, carried out this duty faithfully. Those who received the papers at the bath were illiterate and not in the least interested in the nature of the papers. The policeman himself was illiterate, simple, without malice. He came from Harput and bore no personal hatred toward anyone in Urfa. This plan remained a secret to the very end. At least, no one showed any awareness of it.

During the war, letters passing through the post office were censored. Christians, therefore, began to use biblical references to send political messages to family and friends. Soon Turkish censors discovered this and kept a Bible on hand to decipher the messages. Senders of these letters were arrested. Among the papers which I was asked to translate were letters of this type that the postal censors had overlooked. I was, therefore, careful to place these in the file to be burned.

Just after the Antranig Ferid episode a group of Christian townspeople called upon me to question my methods: "We understand that you are deceiving the government in your work as interpreter. How can you as a clergyman do such a thing?" I do not think they knew about my daily disposition of papers to the bath. They were referring probably to the Ferid papers. And even for this, I do not know the source of their information. The possibilities were several; I did not inquire. Nor did I deny the charge. I explained, "I feel it my duty to save innocent lives and preserve an honorable nation in the only way I can. I do not think it Christian to be a party to murder." They continued, "But don't you realize what will happen if you are caught? Besides, a lie is a lie." I answered, "I am ready to face the gallows, and I will take the risk of going to hell. But, if you insist, I will oblige you by translating everything literally as found, if and when any papers of yours are brought to the court."

They left without any further comment.

16. Officials and Guerrillas

A second occasion to launch an armed defense presented itself early in June within a few days of the first. Even from early times, some Armenians held government positions in Turkey — especially where trust or skill were required. (Sultan Hamid's personal treasurer was an Armenian.) Now as the Turkish plan for solving the Armenian question by annihilation rapidly unfolded, these officials became the target of attacks. In Urfa on June 8, the third mass arrest took place. A group of sixteen Armenians, mainly government officials, were arrested. A few political leaders not arrested with the earlier group were included. Among the officials was Khosrof Dadian, city treasurer. (His arrest was in no way related to the notebook incident.) Among the political leaders were Mgrdich Yotneghparian's three older brothers: Kevork, Nerses, and Hovannes. These arrests added a new dimension to the tensions of the day. Word was received that these prisoners were to be sent to Rakka, a Moslem town about fifty miles southeast of Urfa, near the Syrian border. To what end, no one knew.

Now Mgrdich, very agitated, wanted to start the battle. Disguised as a Kurdish creditor, he visited the prisoners. He offered to break them out of jail and start the battle of defense. The men refused, still believing that armed protest was premature and that their rescue might jeopardize the lives of their families and of the rest of the townspeople. They believed the Mutesarif who had sworn to them on his faith and family that they would all be returned to Urfa within five months. The prisoners again said, "The time to start fighting is when and if an announcement is made that all the Armenians in town are to be exiled." Frustrated once more, Mgrdich had to restrain himself again.

Within two days the prisoners were, as we had heard, transported to Rakka. Their homes were searched, and their wives were questioned in an effort to find hidden guns. None was found. The next week the families of the arrested men were sent to Rakka to join them. We learned that they were treated well at first, and the men and their families were allowed to live in homes in Rakka, but only for about one week. Then the men were jailed again.

Meanwhile in Urfa, on June 25, the Armenian community received a greater shock when the fourth mass arrest took place. Within two hours, in a concerted drive, over one hundred were arrested. This time those arrested were, in addition to the usual political leaders and government officials, the prominent businessmen, tradesmen, and professionals. The following day several of the men exiled to Rakka, including Dadian and Mgrdich's brothers, were brought back to Urfa. So were Antranig Ferid and one of the teachers sent with him to Aleppo. All were returned as prisoners, however. Once more Mgrdich, disguised as a Kurdish creditor, visited the prisoners and made the same offer, to free them and to start the battle of defense. Even after the fourth mass arrest, the answer was the same. "We do not want to be the cause of a massacre by trying to save ourselves." No one in town knew yet that those who had stayed behind in Rakka were marched out into the outskirts of town and killed. There was no direct sign of an impending full scale massacre at Urfa. Mgrdich was stopped a third time.

Continuing orders from Constantinople coming into government headquarters left no doubt that the Armenians of Urfa were destined for annihilation, just like those in other cities. Next on the timetable was a final clean sweep of all remaining Armenian government officials. Locally, among Armenian officials still holding office was Andon Effendi Khoshafian, a friend of my father's from Marash, now a member of the Turkish criminal court in Urfa. I tried to warn him of the coming danger. He chided, "Badveli, my son, the Turkish government does not do anything against the law." He was irritated when I asked, "What laws were being followed during the massacres of 1895 and 1909?"

About a week after the arrest of the one hundred, with no previous warning, all the remaining Armenian government officials of Urfa were dismissed. Thinking that Andon Effendi might listen now, I pleaded with him: "Andon Effendi, do you see now that the Turkish government has no laws? Please, before it is too late, take your family and go to Aleppo. If you stay, in a few days you will be arrested and killed with many others. There is nothing you can do to help matters here." I could not persuade him. He believed that the dismissal was temporary, not a preliminary to arrest. The only mistake I made was in my prediction of the date. He was killed in a month instead of "a few days."

While arrests and harassments continued, Mgrdich, although restrained from starting a direct armed protest, kept his promise to go into hiding and do what he must. With a handful of young guerrillas he kept up a stream of acts of sabotage, providing the only active defense against governmental persecutions. Stories of his daring and resourceful deeds were on everyone's lips. He continued to acquire supplies, weapons, and ammunition for the inevitable battle. With ingenious plans, clever disguises, and bold, dramatic action, he soon became notorious for his activities in Urfa and elsewhere, even as far as Diarbakir and Aleppo.

Once Mgrdich managed to empty out a large cache of valuable rugs confiscated from Armenians in 1895 and stored under guard in the Grand Mosque of Urfa. Disguised as a Turkish official, he approached the guard at the door and demanded that the seal be broken and the door opened. The guard dutifully obeyed. (According to the Turkish custom of the time, a wax seal bearing the insignia of the proprietor or responsible government official used to be placed over the lock on the door of restricted buildings. This was a security measure, and to break such a seal without specific orders from its owner was a punishable crime.) Mgrdich then ordered his men, pretending to be porters, to begin moving out the rugs. The following day Mgrdich and his guerrillas returned and went through the same procedure, emptying out the mosque. Eventually they managed to sell these rugs in distant cities and to use the proceeds for buying guns. Five days after the episode, the real official in charge of these rugs came to the mosque only to discover the place empty. He asked the guard for an explanation. The puzzled guard stated, "Your Honor, you came twice earlier and removed them yourself." The official immediately understood what had happened. "*Mgrdich tekrar oynamish* [Mgrdich has played games again]" was a common expression in town. Official word went out for an intensified effort to capture the imposter. Mgrdich then rode out to the town square, still disguised as a Turk, and with bravado announced, "Who does this Mgrdich think he is? Wherever he is, I'm going to find him!" And off he rode — off to safety.

Mgrdich used the same technique for capturing stores of ammunition and weapons. He and his men, appropriately disguised, rode to the Turkish military encampment at Urfa, unsealed the lock on the depot, and in two days removed quantities of guns. With another daring technique they collected large quantities of Mausers from the fort at Aleppo. Dressed once more as a Turkish officer, Mgrdich assured himself easy access to the interior of the fort. He carefully inspected the premises and located a secret underground passage to the exterior. He devised a plan by which one rainy night his men removed quantities of weapons from the storeroom out through this passage. The theft was not discovered until weeks later, when no amount of investigation could recover the weapons or discover the perpetrators of the deed. Mgrdich and his group were not even suspects.

Nevertheless, in Urfa the Turkish government continued to make every effort to capture Mgrdich and his band. Several times, his home and neighborhood were raided but without success.

Toward the end of June the government began to put pressure on the prelate to find Mgrdich and to convince him and his comrades to surrender. Some of the Armenians believed that if these men were to be surrendered, the confiscations and persecutions would cease. They actually tried to trail the band to turn them in. Although Mgrdich himself was not daunted, his men insisted, after several narrow escapes, that they must leave the city and hide in the caves in the hills near Garmuj — the Armenian town of five thousand just outside Urfa.

In sympathy with Mgrdich's view (that armed resistance should replace appeasement) was Hagopjan Yordoghlian Effendi, another friend of my father's in Marash, and an assistant to the missionaries in Urfa. He had worked for Miss Shattuck and Miss Chambers, and was now working for

Mr. Leslie. Hagopjan Effendi carried messages between Mgrdich and me. Mgrdich and his men knew that I was sympathetic to their view and knowledgeable about government affairs, so they kept me generally informed of their moves, while I passed on whatever information I thought might be helpful for them. Consequently, Hagopjan Effendi brought me word that the guerrillas were planning to go into the hills. I advised against such a plan: "That will not be safe or wise. You will be an easier target there for betrayers." The hills were barren and offered no hiding place other than the caves. There was much traffic in the region, so more danger of observation, especially by the frightened Armenians who wanted to betray them. Hagopjan Effendi understood the folly of the move and carried back the message but returned later with the news: "Badveli, the young people cannot be convinced. They are determined to go into the hills of Garmuj." He and Mgrdich knew better but had to resign themselves to the will of the anxious youths. They could not afford a rift or a separation. They tried to take precautions. Hagopjan himself thought he might be more useful if he went to the village instead of into the hills. He had vineyards in Garmuj, so his presence there would not arouse suspicion. He told me, "I'll bring the boys back. Don't worry."

For several nights Mgrdich transported stores of ammunition to the caves, and finally took his men there — about forty-five of them. The government apparently had already received word of the move. The very next day, on July 6, a group of Turkish gendarmes and soldiers went up to the caves and surrounded the Armenians hiding there. "Come out or you will be killed!" Silence. The Turks then laid down a heavy barrage of gunfire. The Armenians fired back and killed two gendarmes. In a few minutes the Turks realized they would need reinforcements and withdrew out of range, determined to return with a larger force the next day.

The guerrillas were then willing to be led back to the city. Mgrdich always kept a collection of costumes for use as disguises as needed in performing his feats. He and Arush (one of the band) dressed as gendarmes, the rest of the men as Turkish and Arab soldiers. They all walked past the sentries, came into town, and each went into his hiding place. Imagine the disappointment and rage of the large Turkish force that approached the caves the next morning, ready to remove once and for all the chief threat to the success of their official plans! They wreaked all their fury on the poor people of Garmuj. They killed the mayor and several other townspeople. They also killed Hagopjan Effendi. They arrested fifty others and brought them to Urfa. After keeping them in prison for some time, beating and torturing them, the Turks killed all fifty. I personally saw the prisoners being pushed around, cursed, and beaten with the butts of guns. I did not see the worst of the tortures in this episode but could hear the cries of agony drift up from the chambers below.

Only one who has experienced the ordeal or at least seen the results can believe what tortures in Turkish prisons were like — fingernails and toenails pulled out with pliers, hot nails hammered into the head, such vigorous beatings on the back that the raw skin stuck to clothes and was ripped off, boiling hot, hard-boiled eggs fastened under the armpits, eyes gouged from the sockets, tongues cut off, or any other part of the anatomy amputated. Sometimes a prisoner would have several amputations, one at a time, to prolong the agony. These were a few of the common devices, very simple but effective for inflicting excruciating pain.

Two days after the event at Garmuj I went to Hagopjan Effendi's home in Urfa. There I saw only the lad Joseph, the youngest son. He told me all that the guerrillas had done and informed me that his two older brothers, Habib and Francis, had returned with Mgrdich and were hiding in another home. (The oldest brother Dicran was in the Turkish army.)

Government officials were now more than ever determined to lay their hands on Mgrdich and his men. The Turkish authorities, therefore, once more prevailed upon the prelate to order the guerrillas to surrender themselves, giving assurances that no harm would come to them. I begged them not to give themselves up, since I knew that the final word had come: that no one should be spared. But the pressure to surrender for the sake of peace was so strong that, once again, any suspicion of deceit was soon dismissed. Habib, Francis, and a few others of the group, convinced that their lives were no longer in danger, and that they would be relieving the townspeople from further harassment, came out of hiding. Mgrdich and most of his men were not deceived. They remained safe. Those who believed the promises of safety were subjected to severe beatings and killed.

17. Regrouping

U rfa was a regrouping station for exiles — a concentration camp. All summer long caravans of refugees, called "pilgrims" by the Turks, passed through the city. Survivors of the long marches from various Armenian towns were brought here. After Zeitun they came from Furnuz, Albistan, Goksun, and other surrounding towns. They continued to stream in from more distant places — from Harput, from Erzerum, and many more towns. Long, straggling lines of struggling old men; dazed and horror-stricken women; and emaciated, feebly moaning children. Most were in rags — some with no covering at all — weary, hungry and thirsty, stricken with disease, tongues parched, legs swollen, barely able to walk even under the threat of the whip. These were the survivors of original contingents usually ten times as large. Under scorching sun and over burning rocks by day, exposed to wind and dust and insects, with no shelter from the cold, dark nights, they passed through the Valley of Death. No strong young men or beautiful young women could be found in the lines. They had been thoroughly eliminated — kidnapped or killed either before the journey began or on the way.

Remarkable as was the physical survival of these exiles, more remarkable was the spiritual strength that sustained them. Later arrivals told of finding messages on rocks on the way, etched by previous exiles: "We are all headed for death, but let us go courageously. We must not deny Christ, for soon we will go to His bosom." Special verses from the Bible were also written.

The arriving caravans of exiles were gathered into an inn called the Millet Khan near the Turkish armory. Other *khans* were used for overflows. (The khan or caravanserai was the traditional inn for travellers in that part of the world.) The rooms of the Millet Khan were arranged on the second floor, in a row along the full length of one side of an extensive rectangular courtyard. In front of the rooms, from one end to the other, was a wide balcony overlooking the yard below. Underneath the rooms, at one end were the living quarters of the innkeeper, and in the rest of the space were kept the beasts of burden. A high wall enclosed the yard on all four sides. From the side opposite the animals' quarters a gate opened out to the street on this lower level. Another street ran even with the second floor of

64

the khan, and provided direct access to the rooms. The rooms had dirt floors and were dark and dirty. The grounds of the yard were dusty or muddy, generously strewn with dung, garbage, and some straw.

Into the rooms of the khan were crowded, with hardly enough space to breathe, the caravans of exiles. During their confinement in these filthiest of conditions, many more died from starvation, disease, and maltreatment by guards and outsiders. Survivors were once more driven on, this time to Der-el-Zor to perish. The soldiers who escorted these caravans were encouraged to give full sway to their brutal instincts. Once a Turkish official at the court actually told me that ninety-five out of one group of one hundred soldiers who took refugees to the wilderness had themselves died of exhaustion and disease from committing excessive rapes! (Whether this could be true I do not know, but it is significant that the situation could produce such a story.)

Seeing the plight of the exiles from other Armenian cities and hearing their stories still could not convince the Armenians of Urfa that they must fight to save themselves from a similar fate. Rejecting the possibility of exile for themselves, they rushed help to the thousands of refugees brought into the city. Despite the guards and countless other obstacles, every Armenian and Assyrian family brought clothes, food, and whatever else they could, to relieve the suffering of the tortured. Many offered their homes as refuge and concealed their charges from Turkish officials who frequently broke in to search for hidden exiles.

At first, when caravans of exiles came into town, Moslems and Christians went out together to watch the procession. The Christians greeted their fellow countrymen with concern and silent support. They expected the "job" to be finished in a few weeks, after which survivors would return to their homes. Most of the Turks greeted the exiles with what appeared to be quiet admiration and perhaps even a little sympathy in some cases. Soon the outlook was very different. The exiles kept coming and no end was in sight for the tribulations. Moslems were becoming gradually more aroused toward wholehearted dedication to the holy *jihad*. Many soon revealed a mania for wiping out the accursed infidel. The quiet greetings of the Turks were replaced by wild screaming and frenzied shouting as they kidnapped young girls and shot and looted freely. Gendarmes and government officials took advantage of the situation by demanding bribes from Moslems in return for permission to rape and loot without prosecution. Christians no longer dared come out to greet the caravans, though they continued to help unobtrusively in any way possible.

Invaluable in these times were the services of the young Danish missionary Miss Karen Jeppe. She had come to Urfa in 1903 to help in the administration of the German orphanage. This frail person had inexhaustible wisdom and indomitable courage. Sensitive and intelligent, genteel and dedicated, she worked with zest and inspiration. She had learned the Armenian language and studied the history of the Armenians and the

Armenian Church in order to understand her charges better. Throughout the war she served the refugees and the persecuted young men, and saved many from the clutches of the Turk and from hunger. She gave asylum to a group of young Armenian men and repeatedly withstood the raids of Turkish police, protecting her charges with uncommon bravery. During the war I visited her and watched her guard them like a bear protecting its cubs. It was truly remarkable that 100 to 150 Turkish police and soldiers broke into her home over and over, searched everywhere, but never found the place where she had hidden the youths.

On one occasion, Misak, one of her "sons," had come out of his hiding place and was visiting with her. Suddenly Turkish soldiers and police broke in for another search. Misak had no time to return to his hiding place with the other boys, so he quickly dashed upstairs and hid under a pile of quilts stacked in one of the rooms. The soldiers went into the room and stepped on the quilts to see if someone might be there. They felt right and left between the layers and once almost grabbed his foot. Miraculously they did not find Misak. The angel who blinded the evil men gathered at the door of Lot in Sodom likewise blinded the eyes of the murderous Turkish gang. The surprise and joy of Miss Jeppe and the other Armenian boys at this escape had no bounds. In the face of sweeping carnage, saving a single life, even if it might be for a short time, gave cause for genuine thanksgiving.

This raid, like many others, had been instigated by Herr Franz Eckart, a German missionary who had first come to Urfa in 1897 and had originally been very helpful to the Christians but who, after the start of the war, became a collaborator with the Turks and was transformed into an unbelievably cruel demon. I shall tell more about him later, but as far as Miss Jeppe was concerned, he harassed her incessantly to surrender the boys: "You must turn those boys over to the government immediately. The Turks are our comrades in arms. We must not vex them." Eventually Miss Jeppe found it necessary to transfer the boys to her summer residence at a place called Muyejid in the hills near Garmuj. When Herr Eckart intensified his threats, she too went to her summer home and sent the boys one by one to Aleppo to safety.

Karen Jeppe was forced to return to Denmark after the war because of her health. There, too, she did not stay idle. She spoke and wrote everywhere on behalf of the Armenians and in 1920 returned to Syria to give yet more service to her beloved, beleaguered Armenian people. First, she found employment for poor widows. Then, selected for a new assignment under the auspices of the League of Nations, she rescued more than two thousand Armenian women and children scattered among the Arabs of the desert and throughout the small villages of the countryside. She established a hospital for the ill and schools for the children. One orphanage she founded, called Bird's Nest, still operates today (1968) in Beirut under joint Danish and Armenian sponsorship. To the end, she prayed, planned, and worked for the Armenians. Her government honored her most appropriately with its highest medal, Knight of the Legion of

Honor of Denmark. In accordance with her wishes, when Karen Jeppe died, her funeral service was held in the Armenian Apostolic Church.

Another who in these trying times gave varied services in Urfa was Dr. Jacob Kuenzler, a Swiss missionary under the auspices of Dr. Lepsius's Mission of the East. He came in 1899 as a nurse and assistant for Dr. Christ, director of the German missionary hospital, and from 1903 to 1914 under Dr. Andrias Vischer, who replaced Dr. Christ. When the war began, Dr. Vischer was on leave in Switzerland. He was drafted into the army and could not return to Urfa until after the armistice. Dr. Vischer served one more year (1919-20) before returning home to resume his regular medical career. Dr. Kuenzler remained at his post throughout World War I, giving whatever help he could to refugees of all races. His medical services went far beyond those of a nurse, so that he was "Doctor" Kuenzler to all. Eventually, in 1920, while in Switzerland on a one-year leave, he passed examinations at the University of Basle and received his Certificate of Proficiency in Medicine and Surgery, thus becoming, in fact, eligible for the title of Doctor.

Although Herr Eckart tried to prejudice Dr. Kuenzler against the Armenians, and at times it seemed that this missionary acted contrary to the interests of the Armenians, for the most part he tried to serve everyone well. He had learned both the Armenian and Turkish languages as well as Arabic, and was especially adept at dealing with the Turks. Dr. Kuenzler administered contributions received from overseas for the refugees, and in this tried his best to do an equitable job, subject, of course, to Turkish interference.

Mrs. Kuenzler served bravely and enthusiastically together with her husband. After the armistice, they continued their work for many years, primarily with orphans. From 1922 on, they served in Lebanon at Ghazir. In 1925 the Kuenzlers' orphan girls sent a large Isphahan rug to Washington, D.C., in appreciation for help given by the American people through the Near East Relief. The rug measured twenty-three square meters and contained four and a half million knots. Four hundred orphans had woven it over a period of eighteen months.

Concerning the missionary-turned-persecutor, Herr Franz Eckart, much will be told in the course of this story. By way of introduction, he came to Urfa like Dr. Kuenzler, under the auspices of the German Mission of the East. He started as director for a new German orphanage, established to relieve the overload at Miss Shattuck's orphanage. When the number of orphans increased further, Miss Karen Jeppe assisted him. A few years later Eckart devoted part of his time to managing a rug factory (Masmana) established by the mission, assisted there by his wife Emma. Mrs. Eckart was a kind, noble, generous lady who loved the Armenians. But, alas, her sudden, untimely death took her quickly away from her family and from the Armenians. With his wife's support and encouragement, Eckart had happily served the Armenian orphans as a father, and the factory as a kind and able overseer.

Franz Eckart returned to Germany. He remarried. He changed completely. It would appear that he had been recruited by the German government as some kind of agent. Although the second wife, Margaret, was a good wife and mother, she did not have the intellectual and spiritual qualities of Emma, nor did she have any interest in the Armenian people. When Eckart returned to Turkey, it became evident he was filled with a poisonous, fanatical, German nationalism. From then on he was, under the guise of a missionary, a spy among the Armenians. Although he tried to conceal his feelings, he would frequently reveal himself. One day, for example, he scolded the Armenian girls in the factory: "You Armenian girls, not many days from now I'm going to grab you by the hair and hand you over to the Turks!"

When the war started, Eckart stopped going to church. He opened up a *kraat-khaneh* (reading room) for the Turks, which he filled with Turkish and German propaganda books and papers. At the same time, he began cooperating with the Turkish government, encouraging the persecution of the Armenians. His greatest single wish seemed to be the annihilation of the Armenian nation, no doubt so that Turkey could become a province of Germany without the Armenian element of intellectual and economic competition. Eckart could have joined the German army and fought to defend his fatherland. Instead, he stayed in Urfa and robbed and betrayed the defenseless people whom he had previously served for years. Even the Turks were amazed that this man, who had come as a missionary to help the Armenians, could be filled with greater hatred than they and could try even harder to eliminate the Armenians.

As a matter of fact, in spite of official policy, individual Turks here and there tried out of common decency to ease the suffering of their Armenian neighbors. Those townspeople who tried to help the exiles were at first able to succeed in good measure probably because of the relative leniency of the military commander of Urfa — a Syrian Arab, Saduk Bey. He was by nature compassionate, and sympathetic toward the exiles in their plight. He tried to relax the persecution as much as he dared. Within a few months he was dismissed.

I visited the refugees at the khan whenever I could, sheltered some in my home, and generally offered whatever help I could. One visit during the summer of 1915 I shall never forget. It was an especially depressing one. A new group had just arrived. Turkish gendarmes stood guard at the entrance of the inn. A mob of Turkish rogues was gathered out front paying the guards a few cents for each young Armenian woman they could buy to take away. The plight of these girls disturbed even the Turkish gendarmes stationed at the government headquarters. They would say that this brutality was too much, though they did not dare to try to stop the activities. The girls were taken to the vineyards on the outskirts of town, subjected to the most sadistic ordeals imaginable, and buried or abandoned at the end of the "game." Then, back for more girls, more "fun."

I looked around the courtyard of the inn, filled with dead and dying bodies. Turkish workmen collected the bodies — both dead and dying — into garbage carts and dumped them into ditches. Those who were left in the yard as alive were like skeletons who could hardly move. A few of the women had managed to hang on to a few gold pieces. Two Turkish gendarmes, who, I suppose, could have confiscated the money outright, were converting the gold pieces into usable change, but giving only one-half to one-third of actual value in exchange.

Suddenly I saw the crowd stumbling in one direction. Saduk Bey had arrived with a few loaves of bread which he began to distribute to the hungry people. They were falling all over each other to get a piece of bread. Many who fell under foot were unable to rise again. Countless hands were extended toward Saduk Bey. The man was so moved by this scene that he cried out, *"Allah tahir aylesin siz boo haleh getirenleri!* [May God wipe out those who have brought you to this plight!]"

With tears in my eyes I left then, for at that point I could no longer bear the agony of helplessly watching those scenes. On my knees at home I prayed: "Oh my God, You who have placed a limit on the wild waves of the ocean, why have You not placed a limit, also, on the savage crimes of evil and ungodly men?"

18. Kiamilan Imha

On July 10, 1915, four days after the destruction of Garmuj, came the unmistakable signal of full scale massacre: the specific collection of all guns. This was routinely the preliminary step before killing the population of a town. Left with no means of defense, the victims became easy prey. Through the prelate again, an edict was issued for all Armenians to bring all weapons in their possession to the courtyard of the Apostolic church. Anyone disobeying would be severely punished. This order rocked the community as none of the previous harassments had done. The Armenians of Urfa knew that they must not give up their means of defense. Although they abhorred the idea of armed revolt, they preferred — in case of direct attack or threat of forced exile — to die fighting than to surrender to slaughter.

At last Mgrdich Yotneghparian, just back from the caves of Garmuj, could act more freely. In order to gain time, he directed the Armenians to donate their guns — but only those that were defective or broken. These formed a very high mound in the church courtyard. Useful weapons they hid or gave to Mgrdich to store. The Turkish government was somewhat satisfied but suspicious. A search of homes revealed no weapons. In the meantime, Mgrdich had been preparing to fight. He had sent me word saying, "Badveli, Turkish soldiers have started collecting Armenian guns; get ready to resist." (In the plan for defense, I had accepted a place in his group.) I promptly went to my assigned position. But most of the people were still not willing to fight. Men and women from all sides gathered around Mgrdich and implored him to wait a little longer. Urfa might yet escape the fate of other cities. They wanted to wait until the order to leave the city was actually given. He was forced to give in again. We returned to our homes.

An Evangelical brother had seen me at my post and complained to Mr. Leslie. The next day Mr. Leslie invited me to his home for a visit and in the course of the conversation tried to convince me that it was not proper for me as a religious official to carry a gun. To support my stand I cited examples from the lives of Christian individuals and nations, and from the Bible. I then asked him, "Mr. Leslie, if a group of Turks were to come here right now and try to rape your wife, what would you do?" Excitedly he answered, "I'd take this chair and beat them over the head!" I explained, "That is what we are going to do." Mr. Leslie persisted, "You are just a handful of defenseless people; you will all be slaughtered." I answered, "Mr. Leslie, our choice is not whether to die or to live, but rather whether to die honorably or dishonorably." He said no more.

Now that the population appeared to be disarmed, conditions were ready for the next step. Official orders, signed by Talaat Pasha (minister of the interior), came from Constantinople to turn loose a contingent of brutal ruffians to torture and butcher Armenians at will. Two of these monsters — Khalil Bey and Ahmed Bey — came to Urfa from Diarbakir to take advantage of this privilege. Saduk Bey (the local military commander who had brought bread to the refugees at the khan) tried to put a stop to their wild robbing and killing by showing official orders from his superior, Jemal Pasha, military commander of the Fourth Turkish Army with jurisdiction over the provinces of Syria, Lebanon, Palestine, and Arabia. These orders were based on the original decision of the central Turkish government for *kiamilan imha* (to annihilate totally) the Armenians of the Armenian provinces of the Empire, but *kusman imha* (to eliminate only partially) the Armenians in other areas. Since Urfa was outside the boundaries of the Armenian provinces, the military tribunal appointed by Jemal Pasha was proceeding according to the second category. Until the arrival of Khalil Bey and Ahmed Bey, leaders had been imprisoned and harassed, and some local people had been killed. Others had been exiled to Rakka or transported to prisons in Aleppo. But the majority of the populace was as yet unharmed.

When these two fanatics arrived and took charge, they first silenced Saduk Bey by beating him up. They almost killed him. Next, they robbed the Armenians by false promises and extortion. Then they conducted a series of large scale killings.

The Armenians were told that the prisoners (including those returned from Rakka and Aleppo) would be freed and Urfa would be assured its peace and security in return for the payment of six thousand Ottoman gold pieces (about thirty thousand dollars). This was a huge ransom, but worth the sacrifice if we could be sure that the promise would be kept. Naturally, suspicion arose, but let it not be said that the people of Urfa gave any cause for "punishment" or "retaliation." They met the forty-eight hour deadline. Such a flurry of activity! Men, women, and children brought everything they could — rings, bracelets, gold pieces, piled high at the Prelacy. The result: Immediately upon receiving the ransom, the men from Diarbakir, together with a band of local recruits, set to work with relish. Instead of releasing the prisoners, as promised, they tortured them mercilessly, demanding information from them with which to arrest others. The prisoners endured the torture without a single instance of betrayal. The executioners then for a while attacked any Armenian on the streets of the city or on the roads outside. In this manner they killed or seriously wounded two hundred. For days afterwards, the Armenian populace remained in seclusion in its quarter.

The crowning blow came on July 26, when the Prelate Ardavazt was arrested along with forty-one others. Five days later they were all taken to Sheytan Deresi (Devil's Gulch), a ravine a few miles outside the city, near Kara Koepru. Sheytan Deresi was a very convenient place for killings. Hundreds of Armenians were brought there from many areas and slain. Now forty-two more bodies were thrown into the ravine. One more layer of dirt was spread over the corpses by the neighboring farmers. The rings and watches of the slain worn by the murderers were mute witnesses to the crime.

Hardly had this shocking news been realized, when the very next day another crushing blow was struck. On August 1, when I went to government headquarters to translate some letters, I heard some very disturbing news. Zohrab and Vartkes had been brought to Urfa to be killed! Zohrab was an Armenian attorney and a very popular writer. Vartkes was a national leader of the Dashnagtsutiune Party. Both were members of the Ottoman parliament, highly respected by all groups. Zohrab and Vartkes had been among the leaders of the Armenians in the coalition with the Young Turks in the early days. This was the movement that proclaimed "Liberty, Equality, and Fraternity" and promised to save the Empire and to produce a good life for all its inhabitants. Now these two loyal associates of the Young Turks had been brought to Urfa to be killed. The Turks all over town began boasting about the coming execution: *"Istanbuldan iki en beuyik Ermenileri getirdik!* [We brought the two greatest Armenians from Constantinople!]"

I saw Zohrab and Vartkes in the office of the chief of police. I wanted to go near them but found it impossible. They were under heavy guard. Mgrdich made a bold effort to rescue them the night before the scheduled execution. That night Mahmud Nedim Effendi, a notorious sadist and parliamentary representative from Urfa, in order to savor the event to the fullest, invited his two colleagues to be guests at his home. When Mgrdich heard about this, he took two men with him, and at midnight they climbed onto Mahmud Nedim's roof, down the chimney, and into the room where Zohrab and Vartkes were staying. Mgrdich had learned the location of the room through an Armenian woman who worked in the home. He signalled Zohrab and Vartkes to remain quiet and not to be alarmed: "Tomorrow morning you are scheduled to be killed. I have come to rescue you. Get up and follow me." They refused the offer, saying that their escape would bring worse calamity upon the Armenians of Urfa.

The next morning Shakir Bey, the son-in-law of Mahmud Nedim, took time off from his duties on the military tribunal, for which I worked, to lead the group of police officers who took the two men out to Sheytan Deresi and killed them. The following day, members of this contingent were proudly displaying in public the rings and watches of these victims.

Mahmud Nedim was a fanatical Ittihadist nationalist who hated the Armenians. In October, when the Armenians of Urfa were finally being massacred and the whole Armenian quarter was roaring in flames, the cries of infants and mothers rising to the heavens, Nedim was on his balcony, kerchief in hand, dancing, and rejoicing: "Thanks be to Allah, I have seen this day!" Several months later he became totally blind.

19. No More Appeasement

A week after the murder of Zohrab and Vartkes, a new jolt came. Toward the end of July one of the soldiers in the work battalion at Kara Koepru had come to see me. He was a dentist. His commanding officer had sent him to Urfa for a week to make a set of dentures. Arrangements had been made with a local dentist for the use of his office. The soldier told me, "Badveli, in one week we will be killed." That is exactly what happened.

On August 4, 1915, Khalil and Ahmed, taking a group of gendarmes with them, went to Kara Koepru and gave orders to the Armenian (and Assyrian) soldiers working there: "You are now going to work elsewhere. Drop your tools and line up four abreast. Start walking." The soldiers obeyed. About a half hour later, while they were wondering what would come next, Ahmed Bey announced: "I see that some of you are thinking of escaping; I must take precautions and tie you." The soldiers' hands were tied behind their backs, and they were ordered to move on.

When they arrived at Sheytan Deresi, they were suddenly ambushed by a Turkish mob and soldiers who had been waiting there. The shrieking savages began killing the six hundred with bayonets, knives, and axes. The helpless Armenians could neither defend themselves nor escape. Thus, each one was saying his last prayer and falling to the ground like a slaughtered lamb. When the killing started, an Assyrian soldier in the labor battalion begged one of the gendarmes from Urfa whom he knew, "Osman Agha, have pity; at least free us Assyrians." Osman's conscience was touched. He promptly released about thirty Assyrians in the group and saved them from being butchered. One of them was a member of my congregation and my neighbor, Mr. Kachadoor Jamgoch. Two days later he was allowed to return home. Trembling and with tears in his eyes he told me the horrible tale. Kara Koepru (Black Bridge) had now become Kurmuzu Koepru (Red Bridge).

The day after the attack at Kara Koepru the same ambushers went to Kudemma to finish their murderous work. Encouraged by the easy slaughter of the previous day, they started to kill the Armenians at Kudemma without tying them. The Armenian soldiers, using their shovels, started to defend themselves. Several of them wrested guns from Turkish soldiers and were able to shoot their way out to the nearby hills. Soon afterwards, however, after killing the rest of the Armenians who were naturally unable to match the strength of their assailants, the Turks surrounded those who had fled. Only two were able to escape in the darkness. They came to the Armenian quarter in town and described what had happened.

After slaughtering the twelve hundred, the Turks had looted their victims. They had not found much money on their bodies, but in the pocket of each they had found a Bible or prayer book. They had been perplexed momentarily. Then their numbed consciences had awakened somewhat and felt a slight pang. They had buried all the bodies in one pit and all the books in another. (Ordinarily they would have left the corpses out in the open to rot.) Returning into town, they told their story.

Three months later the Turkish government realized that it had forgotten to record any guilt for the twelve hundred. Consequently it fabricated the following crime for the records: "Twelve hundred soldiers who were working near Urfa under the solicitous care of the government ungratefully ran away at night to join the enemy." These were the soldiers who had been brought to Urfa as a labor battalion early in the summer, some of whom had tried to issue a warning to us pointing out the fate of Zeitun, the same soldiers the remnants of whose families we had seen as pitiful exiles on the way to the scorching deserts of Der-el-Zor. The soldiers were finally and permanently united with their families whom the gendarmes had jeeringly "transformed into angels." The massacre of these soldiers alarmed the people of Urfa more than any previous incident. Even some Moslems were apprehensive. "With such extreme injustice we are bringing on the wrath of Allah!" They were, of course, unheeded.

One day Khalil and Ahmed left for Aleppo, and a temporary, brief respite from the massacres came. Jemal Pasha had heard of their activities in Urfa, which were contrary to his policy of *kusman imha* and had ordered them to come before him immediately. It was rumored that Jemal Pasha castigated them and had them shot, and the gold they had collected in Urfa was found in their bags and undoubtedly confiscated by him. We were inclined to believe these rumors because no more was ever heard of them or of the gold.

But the fanatical members of the Ittihad were dissatisfied. So long as Urfa remained under Jemal Pasha's jurisdiction, it would be impossible to exterminate completely the Armenians of Urfa. A petition to Talaat brought about a change of boundaries, and Urfa was placed within the Armenian *vilayet* of Diarbakir. From then on, conditions grew much worse.

Shortly after the boundary change, all the prominent Turks in the city were called to a meeting in the inner chambers of the mayor. Civil and military officials were present, both local citizens and arrivals from Constantinople. I saw them coming out of the meeting, most of the local Turks with disturbed and sad countenances. One of them who did not know me and who seemed to be among the calmer ones stopped by to talk about the session. (I suppose he thought I was a recent Turkish arrival from Constantinople working at the court.) "At the meeting today we heard a top secret order from Constantinople. The government has definitely decided to get rid of all the Armenians. No Turk can spare any Armenian. No room for any personal feelings, because the Fatherland is in great danger. The mayor had each man write the names of his Armenian friends on the official register. That was proof of loyalty. Would you believe it? Some of those men actually wept as they wrote the names."

I froze at my seat. The papers before me suddenly became, for an instant, just a blur. But I quickly regained my composure. Actually, the news should not have been shocking. The plan had been obvious for some time, and the all-out measures were bound to reach Urfa any time. I hoped that now, at least, hearing this official word, my Armenian friends who still believed Turkish promises of friendship would wake up to reality.

By the end of August, all the Armenians of Urfa did finally realize that appeasement and peaceful compliance had brought only increased oppression and gradual elimination of leaders and young men, as well as dwindling of resources. They realized that the pitiable condition of the Armenian refugees from other cities could be theirs, too. Feeling like helpless lambs caught in the jaws of hungry wolves, they were finally ready to accept the defense proposed by Mgrdich. Actually, all hope of survival was lost. The choice was between ignominious exile and murder or an honorable death through active resistance. Almost all of the influential people who had always opposed the decision to resist in the past were already dead. Reverend Akkelian now gave his approval, too. Mgrdich was free to work as he saw the need.

Just at that time a directive came from Constantinople: "Stop the purge of the Armenians at this time; there is a great need for Armenian artisans and workmen to take care of the needs of the troops." Immediately I informed Mgrdich and asked him whether it might not be better to wait during this interval. He answered, "Badveli, the people refused to defend themselves at the right time. Now I don't care whether this is the wrong time or not." He waited for a move from the Turks. The next Turkish aggression against the Armenian community, whatever or whenever it might be, was going to be resisted on the spot. The Armenian youth rallied to the bold, remarkable leader who had become their idol.

Mgrdich and his band were resourceful enough to escape to the south and make it all the way to Basra, where the British were advancing up the Tigris River, but they decided to stay and share the fate of their nation by confronting the Turks of Urfa. Mgrdich had vowed not to allow the Armenians of Urfa to be driven into exile. He meant to keep his promise. Mgrdich, his younger brother Sarkis, Harutiun Rastgellenian, Kevork Alahaydoian, Hovannes Imirzian, Armenag Attarian, and several other young men made final plans for the uneven struggle. Committees were first chosen: military committee, provisions committee, ammunitions committee, and one for tending the wounded and the sick. The Armenian sector was then divided into more than thirty positions and a squad leader appointed for each. Harmony, decisiveness, and trust marked the whole Armenian community. They were ready for a remarkable page in the history of the martyrdom of the Armenian people.

20. A Beautiful Autumn Day

N ear the end of August, 1915, Ismael Bey resigned as chairman of the tribunal. He gave as his reason the pressure of work as director of education, his permanent position in the local government. He was replaced by Shukru Bey, an army major from Constantinople. Though I was prepared for the worst, Shukru Bey proved to be as lenient as Ismael Bey and even more concerned about my personal safety.

Shortly after the new chairman took office, my assistant Ibrahim Fawzil was arrested by the police. Postal censors had found a letter of his to a classmate that they interpreted as revealing the massacre of the soldiers at Kara Koepru. He had written, "Our vineyard in Kara Koepru was eaten by the locusts." Fawzil was rescued from the gallows through the intercession of Shukru Bey.

September 29 was a beautiful autumn day. Early in the morning I finished my pastoral studies and went to the government office to translate the most recently confiscated papers. Shukru Bey greeted me with three bundles: "Preacher Effendi, we brought three prominent men from Aintab. You must translate these papers of theirs so that we can sentence them." When I opened the bundles, I saw with amazement that the men were our respected professors Lootfi Levonian and Lootfi Babigian, and Rev. Kharlambos Bostanji Oghlu. The papers were sermons and lectures. I informed Shukru Bey, "Sir, these writings do not contain a single word relating to politics. I personally know these individuals. They are fine men who serve their country, professionals who are perfectly obedient to their government." Shukru Bey angrily turned to me: "I just lost all my trust in you. What, then, is this map? Isn't it a map of Palestine and Syria prepared for the British?" Reverend Kharlambos believed in the second coming of Christ. He had prepared a map depicting where Christ would come and establish His Kingdom. After a long explanation and much discussion, Shukru Bey was finally convinced that the map of Reverend Kharlambos had no political significance whatsoever.

Soon we had another debate. In one of Professor Levonian's Turkish sermons was a story about a widow who had two children. Shukru Bey said, "See, Preacher Effendi, that widow is your Armenia, and the two children are Turkish Armenia and Russian Armenia, and you want England to be your father." Again I explained that Christian preachers often tell illustrative stories with exclusively religious connotations, never political. After further lengthy discussions, he was finally satisfied that these three men were not dangerous. Shukru Bey had a certain nobility of heart. Therefore, to prevent the murderous gang commissioned by Talaat Pasha from seizing and killing these men anyway, he sent the prisoners that night, guarded by his soldiers, to Aintab, saying, "I will continue their trial in Aintab," and he, too, went there. The two professors were eventually released, but Rev. Kharlambos was transferred to Marash and then killed. I later learned that Shukru Bey did not like the answers the preacher gave at the trial. Why the reverend had to be moved to Marash, I do not know. On the one hand, we rejoiced at the release of the two professors; on the other hand, we were saddened by the martyrdom of the pastor.

Reviewing the papers of the men from Aintab took all morning. When I had finished them, I took a two-hour recess at noon to visit patients at the German hospital at the northeastern end of the Turkish quarter. I had hardly entered the building when the sound of gunfire suddenly erupted from the direction of the Armenian quarter in the west. In a moment, church bells rang loudly and clearly, signalling the start of the Armenian defense of Urfa. Apparently, the Turks had done something, and Mgrdich had started the battle.

With this unannounced, sudden outbreak of fighting I was trapped outside the Armenian quarter. I felt I was going to be seized and killed without having participated in the defense of my people. The glaring irony of my predicament stunned me. I, who had advocated an early stand, was not participating in the defense which had finally begun, while many who had been reluctant to use arms were no doubt now in the forefront of the fighting. My first impulse was to rush home for my gun and then directly to the Armenian quarter across town anyway, but I soon realized the impossibility of such a move then. No one knew, of course, how long the battle would last. Soon we could see from the hospital windows groups of frenzied Turks prowling about the streets shouting for infidel *giavoors* and killing any on sight. Any Armenian in the street would be the certain prey of these hunters. And yet how could I stay in the hospital where there was no way to help my compatriots?

Then I had an intuition. I would report back to work at government headquarters. I might be useful to my compatriots from there. It seemed God was once more guiding me in a direction I had not anticipated. The people at the hospital tried to convince me to stay there. They argued that I would never survive the ten-minute walk which would take me past the Turkish armory and a Turkish bazaar. Even if I did make it through this gauntlet and by some miracle reached the district office, I would be walking into certain death at the hands of the enraged officials. At the hospital I would be safe for a while at least. Nevertheless, I felt compelled to follow my intuition, whatever the risks.

When my work at the hospital was finished, I started out, while my friends sadly and anxiously watched from the hospital windows and prayed for me. In the street I encountered immediately a mob of almost one hundred rioters. With visions of *houris* (heavenly nymphs) as rewards promised by Mohammed, one shouted for Armenians to kill: "Give me ten giavoors to kill with my own hands. I want to have ten houris. Allah, grant me this favor!" Then I heard one of the mob say, as he looked at me, "Aha, a giavoor!" But his companion scrutinized me and said, "This man is not a giavoor; he is an *effendi*. Don't you see how he is dressed? And besides, he does not walk scared." They saluted and made way for me to pass.

As I approached the bazaar, I noticed another roving gang, this a smaller one. Some carried knives that were obviously bloody. I calmly stopped at a booth and began inspecting some merchandise. I was no doubt considered a Turkish Effendi again, as I was left alone. At last I reached the government headquarters alive. In the courtyard I saw a motley group of Turks gathered around the bodies of two Turkish policemen slain by Armenians. The Turks were shouting all kinds of insults and curses on the Armenians and were vowing to put to the sword all the Armenians of Urfa. As I passed by, I remarked, "What a pity that two such young men should be killed . . ." Thus, I was not conspicuous for having ignored the corpses, and I arrived at my offices safely.

When I entered the courtroom, Shukru Bey approached me saying, "Son, you Armenians are making a big mistake. You are going to bring about the total destruction of your quarter and your own annihilation. I am truly sorry." Prudence required that I remain silent. This was not the place for debate. I believe he really was sorry. I was, in fact, grateful that he showed concern and not outright hostility. We proceeded with our routine reviews. After I had completed my assignments for the day, Shukru Bey further showed his personal concern when he offered me the choice of being a guest in his home or of going to my own home in the Assyrian quarter under the protection of an assigned guard. I gratefully chose the latter. A Turkish soldier escorted me home. Shukru Bey sent word to my Turkish neighbor, Atesh Bey, holding him responsible for my safety. In truth, his sons gave me excellent protection. Their mother, Gulamdan Hanum, was an especially kind woman who made sure that the boys did their job well. She lamented, "My heart grieves when innocent people, especially women and children, are killed." Her tender heart could not stand the strain of that month. Sad to say, she died soon after.

During the twenty-five days of the battle I was allowed to carry on my pastoral and governmental duties. I asked the officials permission to keep the Assyrian church open: "Six days a week I serve you; the seventh let me serve God." They let me do so, and the congregation was most grateful. Occasionally I was able to help refugees who were outside the embattled areas.

One day as I was leaving home, two Armenian women, a young girl, and two boys appeared in the street. They had left the refugee *khan* and had wandered toward the Assyrian part of town, as they sought shelter. The women were sisters from Mezire, Mrs. Elmas Kezirian and Mrs. Loosaper Nahigian, both widows, the latter being the mother of the children — Angel, Edward, and Tsolag. I took them into my home. One of my Assyrian neighbors, seeing them, began shouting from the rooftop for my arrest and the seizure of the refugees. This neighbor, called Lavlav Tumo, was an erratic fellow, a character both pitied and ridiculed by the community. Apparently he was panic-stricken. He was afraid that if the government were to find out that I was harboring Armenians, all the neighbors would be punished for not having turned me in. Tumo's family quickly brought him down from the roof. When Gulamdan Hanum heard the commotion, she sent her oldest son to help. He assured Tumo that all would be well, and he stood guard at my home all that night. Tumo gave no further trouble. Aside from Atesh Bey, everyone else in the neighborhood was Assyrian, so nothing came of this incident.

Mrs. Nahigian was ill and near the end of the month needed hospitalization. Using a coffin available from church, the two Turkish boys and I carried her to the hospital. That was the only way we could get her there safely. Unfortunately, she could not be saved. The children and their aunt eventually found refuge in America.

2. *City of Marash before the First World War.*
(From the volume Marashi patmutiun.*)*

3. *Ebenezer Orphanage.*
(From the volume Marashi patmutiun.*)*

4. City of Tarsus, ca. 1909.
(Zoryan Institute Photo Archives.)

5. Administration building, St.
Paul's College.
(Zoryan Institute Photo Archives.)

6. Model of St. Paul's College administration building built by Reverend Jernazian, the "carpenter."
(Jernazian family collection.)

7. *Dr. and Mrs. Thomas Christie.*
(Zoryan Institute Photo Archives.)

8. *Miss Agnes Salmond.*
(Jernazian family collection.)

9. *College orchestra, St. Paul's*
College, Tarsus, ca. 1913.
(Jernazian family collection.)

10. *Armenian refugees, courtyard*
of St. Paul's College, during the
1909 massacre in Tarsus.
(Zoryan Institute Photo Archives.)

11. *A section of the city of Adana, before the 1909 destruction.*
(Zoryan Institute Photo Archives.)

12. *Same section of Adana, soon after the 1909 events.*
(Zoryan Institute Photo Archives.)

13. *Class of 1914, Marash Theological Seminary.*
First row, left to right, *Ephraim Jernazian, Sarkis Chobanian;*
center row, left to right, *Reverend Garabed Harutunian, Reverend Simon Terzian, Dr. Fred Goodsell, Reverend Woodley;*
back row, left to right, *Kevork Sahagian, Nerses Sarian, Simon Vehabedian, Asadour Solakian, Siragan Agbabian, Dickran Antreasian, and Harutun Nokhoudian.*
(Jernazian family collection.)

14. *Marash Theological Seminary.*
(From the volume Marashi patmutiun.*)*

15. *City of Marash, the American compound at upper right section.*
(Zoryan Institute Photo Archives.)

16. *City of Urfa.*
(Zoryan Institute Photo Archives.)

17. *Marie Jernazian.*
(Jernazian family collection.)

18. *First from left, Marie Jernazian*
(then Hovagimian) at graduation.
(Jernazian family collection.)

19. *First Armenian Protestant Church of Urfa.*
(Courtesy of Rev. Jacob Iwaz.)

20. *Entrance to old Assyrian Protestant Church in Urfa.*
(Courtesy of Rev. Jacob Iwaz.)

21. *Armenian Apostolic Church in Urfa.*
(Courtesy of Rev. Jacob Iwaz.)

22. *Armenian compound in Urfa.*
(Courtesy of Rev. Jacob Iwaz.)

Մկրտիչ Եօթնեղբարեան

23. *Mgrdich Yotneghparian*
(Courtesy of Satenig Yotneghpar-
ian.)

24. *Skeletal bones of unburied victims of the Genocide; the photograph that*
was used to arrest Reverend Jernazian.
(Jernazian family collection.)

Part III
The Battle of Urfa and
Its Aftermath

21. The Battle

The story I am about to relate is based on details gathered from government offices, from members of my Assyrian congregation who were drafted to build ramparts for the Turks, from Armenian survivors in the battle zone, and from my own personal observations. (I joined others at the district headquarters in watching the various operations through binoculars.)

Early in the afternoon of September 29, a group of Turkish police and soldiers marched into the Armenian quarter on one of their random expeditions of harassment and surrounded the Saderjian home, under the usual pretext of searching for Armenian military deserters. Instead of entering through the front door, they knocked a hole in the roof and began to break in from above in order to shock and terrorize the occupants of the house. It so happened that Mgrdich Yotneghparian and his band were in that house. The first policeman at the hole was shot before he could enter. The soldiers outside then began to shoot at the house from all directions.

This was the incident for which Mgrdich had waited. He sent word through underground tunnels to give the signal that the battle of resistance by the Armenians of Urfa was to begin. The signal was the ringing of the church bells. These bells had been silent for many years. The last time they had been heard was in December of 1895. The Turks had suddenly rung them then at an unscheduled hour to announce the beginning of the massacre that year. While most of his neighbors ran for cover on that occasion, thirteen-year-old Mgrdich had joined a group of defenders who had taken a position at the Ketenjian residence. He had climbed to the roof and with his slingshot cast rocks down upon the frenzied Turks. He also fetched ammunition for the fighters. The incident made a very deep impression on him. He dreamed of the day when the Armenians themselves would ring that bell as a prelude to a strike at the Turks.

Now, twenty years later, that day had come. The bells of the two Armenian churches began to ring. Mgrdich's younger brother Sarkis rang the Apostolic church bell; another young lad rang the Protestant church bell. The two boys then began to sing out patriotic songs from the church steeple, to encourage everyone to fight with a song and to die heroically rather than be massacred amidst weeping and wailing. People responded

83

immediately and occupied their assigned positions. The era of peaceful effort was over. The time for action had come.

The Armenians at once seized the police and the gendarmes in their midst, took away their guns, and launched the uneven battle, happy that they could die honorably, defending their own homes. These defenders were only a handful of untrained young people, supported by old men and women and children accustomed only to peacetime activities. Other than Mgrdich and his guerrillas, there were no trained fighters to carry on the battle and very few community leaders left to furnish guidance.

The Turkish government took two steps. First, it surrounded the Armenian quarter with all the military force at hand and with volunteer reinforcements. Then the *mutesarif*, Ali Haydar Bey, sent a reassuring letter to the Armenians, saying, "The government has no evil intentions toward the Armenians. The police made a mistake. Have no fear. Let everyone resume his usual activities. Move about freely." Mgrdich wrote in reply, "Honorable Ali Haydar Bey, after the numerous deceptions that brought arrests and killings, we no longer can have any trust in the Turkish government. We have, therefore, resolved to die honorably rather than submit to being trapped and slaughtered."

The night passed in silence. The Armenians began setting up barricades everywhere and preparing to surprise the Turks with hard fighting. In the morning the Turks arrived expecting to carry out a massacre as in 1895. They began attacking from several positions. The lone voice of one Moslem priest was heard pleading, "Moslems, it is a sin to kill innocent Armenians; it is against the law of Allah. They are our obedient subjects."

On rare occasions Moslem clergy had the courage to speak thus against the massacres. The plea of this priest was reminiscent of a similar incident at Konia where the head of the peaceful Mevlavi sect, Chelebi Zadeh, had cried out, "The Armenians are the roses of Allah and prophet Jesus Christ. Do not kill them. It is a sin." Though the massacre at Konia continued, the epithet "roses of Allah" was reiterated sporadically from then on, even by simple Turkish peasants who could see no reason to kill their friendly Armenian neighbors. But the frenzied mobs would not be stopped anywhere.

The gangs in Urfa ridiculed the priest and advanced toward the Armenian quarter to loot and kill. Mgrdich waited until they had been lured sufficiently deep into the quarter to make retreat costly, then attacked. The Turks sustained heavy losses before withdrawing. Stunned by this unexpected defense, they sought help from neighboring towns and from the military chief at Aleppo.

Just at that time the Armenians of Musa Dagh had succeeded in escaping the clutches of the Turk after weeks of heroic resistance. Fakri Pasha, the Turkish military leader of the forces that fought there, was ordered to proceed to Urfa to take over control of the "revolt." He had been joined by Kalib Bey and the German Votsgield and his contingent. Within a week they arrived with a force of six thousand trained troops. Throughout that week the Turks at Urfa, assisted by nearby Moslem tribesmen, had made repeated attacks upon the Armenians but had been repulsed each time, suffering heavy losses. Fakri Pasha's troops arrived on October 6. The local Turks, who had gathered at the cemetery just outside the city, met them with jubilation.

Mgrdich's brother Sarkis and six other Armenian young men had put on Kurdish garb and mingled with the Kurdish and Turkish mobs awaiting the arrival of the soldiers. The troops began advancing toward the Armenian quarter. In front came the cannon with one or two soldiers seated on each one. Shots suddenly rang out, and the soldiers on one cannon toppled over. There was great consternation in the ranks. By the time the Turks realized that the disguised Armenians had done the shooting, the boys had removed the pin from the cannon and fled over the hill and returned to their positions. The mission was successful. The arrogance and confidence of the Turks were shattered.

Before launching an attack, Fakri Pasha first tried to beguile the Armenians into surrendering. He wrote to Mgrdich, praising his valor and promising that, if the Armenians surrendered, there would be no punishment; if not, the whole Armenian quarter would be reduced to rubble. After consulting with his colleagues, Mgrdich decided not to be fooled by the usual Turkish lies but to fight to the end. He sent word to Fakri Pasha suggesting that they might discuss the matter if Fakri Pasha would come to the German rug factory so that Mgrdich might speak to him from the house across the way. The Pasha agreed and came. He began with mild, sweet tones: "My children, why are you rebelling against your government? The government has no evil intentions toward you. Spare your wives and children, and surrender." Mgrdich answered, "Pasha Effendi, we have never rebelled; on the contrary, we have been your most obedient subjects. Yet you kill us and want to annihilate us. Pasha Effendi, I have three questions for you. Answer these satisfactorily, and we will put down our guns. You arrested, imprisoned, and mercilessly killed our prelate and our elders. Why? You called for military service thousands of our young men to serve the Fatherland, and they served with perfect loyalty; yet you cruelly destroyed them. Why? More than twelve hundred Armenian soldiers were working obediently at Kara Koepru and Kudemma; you butchered those loyal soldiers, too. Why? Fakri Pasha, if you cannot answer these questions, let the local authorities answer."

There was dead silence. Mgrdich continued, "Fakri Effendi, let us not try to fool each other. You have come to massacre us, and we have decided to die defending ourselves honorably." Fakri Pasha jeered angrily, "Then you will be responsible for the misfortunes that will befall your wives and children!"

Heavy attacks began from all sides. The Armenians drove back the attackers at all points, inflicting heavy losses. The Armenian young men shouted across the barricades to the auxiliary Turkish soldiers, "You out-of-towners, go away and let the brave Turks of Urfa, who killed our soldiers with their hands tied, attack us. Let the officials who extracted thousands of gold pieces from us with false promises attack us." Sometimes the Armenians threw gold coins out into the street and taunted, "You want to confiscate our gold; come and get it. Why don't you come?"

The battle lasted almost a month. The first week the Armenians with clever strategy devised by Mgrdich lured large numbers of the enemy into traps and inflicted heavy losses on them. During the second week the six thousand regular soldiers of Fakri Pasha plus the more than ten thousand Moslem (Turkish, Kurdish, and Arab) volunteers from Urfa and the surrounding areas made very heavy attacks. The Armenians managed to keep their positions, but by the third week were considerably weakened. In spite of the overwhelming odds against them, the Armenians fought resolutely. Their heroic deeds alone could fill a large volume. A number of times Mgrdich's tactics called for infiltration of enemy sectors by Armenians in disguise, to gather information or to create disruption. His men carried out these assignments without hesitation and successfully. Besides inflicting losses on the enemy, these clever tactics helped the Armenians acquire weapons from the Turks and prolonged their ability to resist.

Only about fifty young men, most of them Mgrdich's guerrillas, were trained in the use of weapons. Some young women as well as other young men were given brief training during the last days of preparation. Most of the fighters were untrained civilians who followed instructions and fought with courage. Actual fighters numbered only about three hundred. The Armenian quarter was divided into thirty-two sections. About ten fighters were assigned to each section under the command of a "corporal" and his assistant. Each squad had a courier by which it kept in touch with headquarters. Mgrdich and six lieutenants circulated from post to post directing the strategy, maintaining discipline, and giving encouragement. Those who did not have weapons served in countless other ways. Generally, older men prepared hand grenades and ammunition. Older women cared for the children. Young women cared for the sick and wounded and kept up morale with patriotic songs and exhortations. A number of young women, including Mgrdich's sister Mariam and wife Elizabeth, joined in the actual fighting as the ranks diminished. Others took care of the daily necessities of food and other supplies. Young boys and girls eagerly performed whatever errands they were called upon to do. They carried messages, manned observation posts, delivered supplies, and at the end also fought.

The Turks, on the other hand, often retreated quickly when faced with resistance. In fact, Turkish officers were seen shooting at their own men at times, to stop them from running away. But, of course, they had overwhelming advantages in numbers and supplies.

By the end of the third week Armenian grenades and bullets were fast being used up. There were not enough people to replace the dead and wounded. The enemy was receiving steady reinforcements in men and ammunition. The Armenians had only hand weapons. The Turks had two cannons at first, and four more were brought in from the outside. By October 9 all six were in use. Placed in pairs at three strategic locations — the citadel, Telfedur Hill, and the hill behind St. Sarkis Monastery — they kept up a steady barrage of shellfire from three directions until the Armenian quarter was demolished. Although several fighters made heroic efforts to sabotage these cannon, and were partially successful, they could not hope to destroy them completely.

The Turks received invaluable aid from the German missionary Herr Eckart. When they were having difficulty aiming their cannon at strategic points in the Armenian sector, Herr Eckart, being a trained artilleryman, came to their aid. He most effectively directed the shellfire, demolishing the Armenian positions one by one. Especially ironical was his merciless shelling of the beautiful Armenian Evangelical Church. This impressive building had been built in 1880 through the efforts of the pastor, Rev. Hagop Abuhayadian (martyred in 1895). Kaiser Wilhelm I had donated one thousand dollars to the building fund. Herr Eckart himself had worked in that church. He was now destroying the building, killing hundreds of innocent people gathered there, weeping and praying in the sanctuary.

The plight of the Armenians worsened consistently as leaders were wounded. On October 9, right after an unusually successful skirmish, Mgrdich was wounded. His right knee shattered by shrapnel, he was no longer able to make his rounds. For two weeks he still gave directions and encouragement from the basement where he was confined. Eventually, all the leaders were killed or wounded.

Just before the last concentrated bombardment, the German officer Voltsgield warned Mr. Leslie that the mission would no longer be spared and suggested it be vacated. Until then, that complex was safe from attack. Under a truce then, Mr. Leslie evacuated most of the orphans and foreign internees (who had sought refuge there) to the safety of the St. Sarkis Monastery or to buldings in the Assyrian quarter. But he and fourteen other internees refused to abandon his mission compound and stayed until the very end. Finally, on October 18, at Mgrdich's request they raised a white flag and left. The Turks interned them at a *khan*. Armenians dressed as Turks then entered the mission and made one last successful attack against a contingent of fifty Turks who followed them in, thinking they were fellow Turks. By October 23 the battle was over.

The final ordeal came when the Turks broke through the barricades and pushed into the heart of the Armenian quarter. To avoid falling into the hands of Turks, some shot their wives, children, and themselves. Some piled their furniture in one room and, lighting a fire to the heap, threw themselves as a family into the flames. Others threw themselves into wells. Some hid in underground passages but often were found and slain.

Mgrdich committed suicide at the last minute to avoid being taken prisoner. His body was found by the Turks and was paraded through the streets of the city. As for Sarkis, he was in a wounded and semi-conscious state when he fell into the hands of the Turks. They took him to a hospital and later hanged him. Of the fighters who remained alive and were arrested, seventy were hanged in the three public squares of the city. One of those hanged was Rev. Solomon Akkelian. He was of strong physique. While he was being hanged, the rope broke. Turning to his executioners he said disdainfully, "Ottomans, everything you do is as rotten as this rope." According to Turkish custom, the one being hanged was set free whenever the rope broke. In this instance, the Turks paid no attention to their custom. They hanged the pastor with a new rope.

One of the Yotneghparian brothers — Levon — survived the war. He had been drafted into the Turkish army and was absent from Urfa during the war years. One of the few Armenian soldiers who were not murdered, he settled in Marseille in France after the war. In World War II he was killed by a German sniper's bullet one morning when he stepped out of his home.

Mariam Yotneghparian died defending the position at the Apostolic church. Elizabeth was captured and, together with several others, was sentenced to 101 years in prison. She was released when the British occupied Urfa after the armistice. Elizabeth made her way to her brother in New York in 1919. But she was so troubled over the ordeals she had been through that she had to be placed in a psychiatric hospital in 1926, where she remained until the end. Elizabeth's mother and infant son were exiled and perished in the desert.

Let me mention one recorded story of the experiences of some of the Armenian survivors in the aftermath of the battle. With repetition, the details may have become embellished for dramatic effect, but there is no reason to doubt the basic facts or the prevailing spirit of savagery. Just as there were a few *mullahs* (Islamic religious mentors) who considered the massacres a sin, there were other mullahs who were murderers and sadists. The Turks herded many Armenian women and children into the courtyard of the Apostolic church before their final disposition. A mullah, escorted by two soldiers, came in and wielding a sword in his hand he announced, "Listen, you *giavoors*. Last night in my dreams I saw the prophet Mohammed. He ordered me to sacrifice 100 Armenian male children under one year of age in your sanctuary at the altar." Whereupon, his escorts circulated through the courtyard seizing infants from the mothers' arms and delivering them to the mullah. He decapitated the babies one by one in front of the altar. He rested at the end of the 50th, then resumed his sacred work. When he had completed the 99th decapitation, the sword flew out of his hand, and he collapsed. His final words as he died were, "Oh Allah, you should not have demanded more than this from your servant!"

As for the rest of the Armenian survivors, 250 were shot and 250 were bayoneted in public executions. Hundreds of young girls and women were taken to Turkish homes as slaves, or out of town where, after being subjected to unspeakable, savage ordeals, they were killed and thrown into ditches. Most of the Armenians who had been permanent residents of the Armenian quarter were either killed, exiled, or committed suicide. Those surviving Armenians who were refugees from other towns were not included in the brutal attacks. In keeping with the original disposition planned for them, they were returned to the khan before deportation to the desert.

The heroic Battle of Urfa remains a unique page in the annals of human valor. Where else in history have a handful of untrained boys and girls fought so bravely against such great numbers of trained troops and seasoned, savage plunderers? At Thermopylae the small band of fighters in the uneven battle were trained Greek soldiers under an experienced leader, Leonidas. The immortalized "Light Brigade" at Sevastopol was composed of the most highly trained soldiers of the British Empire. The bravery of the defenders of Urfa remains unmatched.

22. Abandoned Property

After defeating the Armenians, the Turkish troops and ravenous mob had poured through the Armenian quarter and within two days had finished devastating what the Armenians had built and rebuilt for two thousand years. From the minarets the Turks praised Allah for this wonderful opportunity.

Several days after the massacre, two old Turks were walking through the street. One of them, turning to the other, remarked, "We were wrong in killing the innocent Armenians. May Allah forgive us." The other, stroking his beard, said, "I felt sorry for them, too, especially for the killing of the women and children and wrecking of their homes. In a way, though, the Armenians deserved this punishment because I hear they wore fezzes without black bands and they rode horseback and passed ahead of Turks."

Among the victims of this battle was Mr. Leslie. Ever since the beginning of the war in 1914, he had been under constant harassment. The Turkish government, supported by Herr Eckart, tormented him more and more as they also escalated their persecution of the Armenians. Frequently they concocted accusations charging him with sending to Washington consular reports condemning the Turks. Actually, Mr. Leslie was too eager to avoid trouble; he was not the sort of person who would stir up agitation by writing such incriminating reports.

During the summer of 1915, Mr. Leslie's wife had gone to the hospital at Aintab where their first child was born. Dr. Kuenzler and others convinced Mr. Leslie that he would not be neglecting his duties if he were to take a little time off to be with his wife and new child. On the day that he was scheduled to leave, the Battle of Urfa began. He remained at his mission post in the Armenian quarter, refusing even to move to the safer Assyrian quarter. After the battle Mr. Leslie was allowed to live at the Kuenzler home but was required to report daily at government headquarters, where the officials continued to pressure him with interrogations and threats. On October 30, Mr. Leslie did not make it back to the Kuenzler residence. His lifeless body was found in the street near the German hospital. The following note was said to have been found on him:

My last Testament.
No one in Urfa is any way responsible for my action except myself. Specially the family of Mr. Kuenzler and Eckart are not involved in the thing that I have done. What I have drunk, I have brought from the building of the mission. I am not implicated in the Armenian revolution but was brought under by it.
F.H. Leslie

I personally doubt the authenticity of this note for a number of reasons. The original was never produced, not even when the American missionary, Dr. Merrill, came to Urfa in 1916 to have a gravestone erected for Mr. Leslie. Only a copy was publicized. I was never called to translate this document, in spite of the fact that, as official government interpreter, I was always called to translate documents relating to American missionaries. Why would Mr. Leslie choose a filthy street in which to commit suicide rather than his own home or American missionary headquarters? Why would he make a specific point to indicate that Kuenzler and Eckart had no part in his death? Why use the title "Mr." for Kuenzler and none for Eckart, when the latter was generally considered to have higher rank and therefore to be entitled to a more formal title? Furthermore, I knew Mr. Leslie very well from my stay at the Marash Theological Seminary, where he lectured to us, and I was in constant touch with him in Urfa for a year. The English in this note does not resemble his English. In addition to the poor construction of the language, the use of the term "revolution" was not typical of Mr. Leslie. He used "self-defense," whereas the Turkish government and the Germans used "revolution."

The Armenian community remained for the most part skeptical of the verdict of suicide. But questions could not be raised openly at the time. Suspicions had to remain private. Dr. Kuenzler, certainly not interested in gaining the hostility of the authorities, recalled some comments Mr. Leslie had made indicating his concern and frustration over the intolerable condition of the Armenians. Dr. Kuenzler and other foreign missionaries readily accepted the verdict of suicide. I still believe the Turkish government and Herr Eckart buried the truth with Mr. Leslie.

Most of the Turks had no qualms about the slaughter at Urfa. Their next item of business was the appropriation of the confiscated property of the Armenians. Many Turks took home the surviving children to find out where the parents had hidden their money and other valuables. After forcing the children to show the hidden property, the Turks killed the Armenian youngsters. Herr Franz Eckart participated in the looting and also devised new plans to annihilate more of the Armenians.

Just before the battle, when the Armenians were convinced that they would be deported as were their compatriots in other cities, they looked for safe places to deposit their money, jewelry, and other valuables — with the hope of possible recovery sometime in the future. Some families concealed the items in their homes; some had faith in the Ottoman Bank; many entrusted their possessions to Mr. Leslie; some to Dr. Kuenzler; and a great number gave theirs to Franz Eckart for safekeeping. Herr Eckart himself solicited this service, and after convincing the Armenians to place their belongings into his hands, also advised them to take refuge in the rug factory sponsored by the German missionaries, in order to avoid exile. Many still believed in his sincerity. They were not yet aware of his transformation from a genuine, helpful missionary to a fanatical enemy. About one hundred Armenians gave him everything and moved into the factory, never suspecting the fiendish plot Eckart had for them.

Herr Eckart's coffers were filled with the money and jewels of the Armenians, and his factory was filled with valuable goods as well as their owners. It was not long before Eckart locked the door of the factory, took the key to the Turkish government, and made them an offer: "A group of Armenians has occupied our factory; take the key and deport them." The Turkish soldiers drove all the Armenians who had taken refuge there out into the desert. Most of the exiles died. A few women survived and returned. When they asked Herr Eckart to give at least one gold piece from the hundreds they had given him for safekeeping, he beat them away, scolding, "You Armenians have no right to live, let alone ask for the return of your money."

The day after he had betrayed the Armenians to the Turks, Franz Eckart returned buoyantly to the factory to begin to classify and sell his booty. When he reached a corner of the building where there was an abandoned well, he noticed that there were two Armenians hiding there. Eckart angrily ordered them to come out. They paid no attention to him, knowing that coming out meant death by torture, while staying till night held out some hope for escape. When Eckart saw that they would not obey his order, he piled heavy steel weights over the top, and with the verdict "Then I will make this well your grave," he covered the opening and went home.

Franz had a younger brother, Herr Bruno Eckart, who was exactly the opposite in temperament. Bruno was very kindhearted and full of love and sympathy for the Armenians. He was powerless, however, to influence Franz. Brokenhearted after a visit to Franz's home later that same day, Bruno stopped at the factory. He heard the cries for help coming from the two Armenians in the well. Bruno immediately went to Miss Jeppe and with her permission moved the Armenians to her home. After having rested there for some time, the two were able to leave the town disguised as Arabs, and to escape the clutches of Franz Eckart.

Herr Eckart sold part of his stolen goods in Urfa through a Turk called Ahmed Agha. The rest he gradually transported to Aleppo and sold from there. At first he proceeded unhampered, because he enjoyed the protection of the local German military director who shared in the loot. By 1918 conditions had changed. When Eckart learned that Germany was losing the war and was about to surrender, he immediately started to make plans for escaping out of Turkey. On one of his trips to Aleppo, while transporting seven cartloads of goods, Eckart was arrested by the Turkish government and imprisoned for having stolen Armenian money and possessions, *emvalu metrookeh* (abandoned property), which rightfully belonged to the

Turkish government. I was at headquarters when those goods were brought in at Urfa. I verified their being Armenian goods; many items still bore the names of their owners. But Eckart knew the temperament of the Turks. Through one of his friends he bribed the *mutesarif*, the chief of police, and a few other officials, and escaped. When he reached Constantinople after the armistice, the British, having no doubt received information about him in advance, arrested him as a murderer and a thief. I received a newspaper from Constantinople then in which there was an article about his arrest, including my name and that of Armenag Abuhayatian as witnesses of his crimes. I do not know how we happened to be named. Eckart had denied everything and sworn that he never knew us.

Again bribing prison officials, Eckart managed to escape from prison. But he was shot down while crossing the border. It was impossible to verify who killed him. Thus Eckart eventually forfeited to the Turkish government the Armenian properties he had appropriated for himself, and he lost his own life. Although his wife and children did reach Germany, they had some very difficult times, and each one reached an unfortunate end. The eldest son Martin died very soon after reaching Germany. The rest worked in menial jobs to survive. Mrs. Eckart soon became ill and died. Elizabeth married Dr. Lepsius's son, but shortly afterward both contracted tuberculosis and died. None of the others was married. All died young.

Two weeks after the end of the Battle of Urfa, the second chief of the military tribunal, Shukru Bey, left. Another local chief with the same name as the first one, Ismael Bey, who had been *jeza reisi* (head of the civil criminal court), took over the leadership of the military court. Possibly anticipating support from this new chief, the same Captain Ramzi Bey who had earlier tried to attack Antranig Ferid, one day challenged my faithfulness as an interpreter: "During all this time you have not translated a single piece of pernicious writing." I made a counter-challenge: "Ramzi Bey, you are the ones who search the homes. Whatever you bring me, that is what I translate." Promptly Ismael Bey and Shakir Bey chastized him, and from then on he did not criticize again. I found the new Ismael Bey basically a kindhearted fellow. He was a Cypriot who liked the Armenians and was not at all in favor of the persecutions. He carried out his official duties as required, but remained as tolerant as his office would allow. In time, he was to save my life.

In the aftermath of the Battle of Urfa I received an additional assignment. In November of 1915 the Turkish government, by central directive, confiscated the money and jewels left by Armenians at the Ottoman Bank and with the now dead Mr. Leslie. Also, the officials closed the Armenian stores and placed government seals on the doorlocks, to prevent looting and eventually to sell the goods left there and keep the proceeds. The stores and shops of the Armenians were in the central shopping area of the city, so were still intact. The shattered Armenian quarter never included any business establishments.

To implement the appropriation of property, a committee arrived from

Constantinople — Emvalu Metrookeh Tevziyeh Komosiyonu (Commission for Disposition of Abandoned Properties). This commission was to sell the "abandoned" properties of the Armenians, and to collect the outstanding bills of Armenian merchants and pay their debts. Since almost all the account books were in Armenian, I was called to translate them into Turkish. The commission first designated one of the government buildings as its headquarters and furnished the rooms with valuable rugs and furniture taken from Armenian homes. The commission then went through the formality of announcing to the Turkish inhabitants that any who had money to collect from the Armenians should present their petitions to headquarters. More than two thousand bills were presented, most of them false. It did not matter because to this day, I am sure, not one cent has been paid, neither to legitimate nor illegitimate claims.

The commission began its work of disposition by breaking into Armenian stores one by one and selling their contents at auction. The chairman of the commission, Nabi Bey, took me with him so that I could keep a record of the merchandise sold. With us were two policemen and an auctioneer. The ritual was the same at each store. First they examined the door seal, then broke it. Next they forced the door open, and then put up the merchandise for auction. Neither the sellers nor the buyers knew the actual value of the goods. As a result, items would sell for many times their worth, or conversely, many times less than they were worth. No one was concerned about accurate appraisals. In the evening Nabi Bey took the account records home with him. At night he juggled the accounts, pocketing a share of the proceeds. The following day, when I saw the recorded entries in the office files, the figures were in his handwriting — not my originals — and the amounts altered. Actually we found relatively little in these stores because the local government officials would enter these buildings at night through a hole made in the roof or a wall, and they would steal a large share of the goods.

One day several German and Turkish merchants came to buy some rugs which had been confiscated from Armenian homes and locked up in the Armenian Catholic Church. A corporal and four gendarmes kept watch there day and night. When we went there with the merchants and Nabi Bey, inspection of the door seal showed the label "Ishmael." No one knew who Ishmael was. Nabi Bey ordered the seal broken and the door opened. We found not a single rug in the church. In amazement Nabi Bey asked the corporal, "Where are the rugs?" The corporal answered, "Bey Effendi, no rugs were entrusted to me, just the seal on the door, and you have seen that the seal has been kept unharmed." Investigation revealed that a group of Turkish officials regularly went there at night, opened the door, stole some rugs, closed the door resealing it with the name "Ishmael" — and, of course, giving the guards a share of the goods.

One day when I walked into the committee room, I noticed that the valuable rugs and drapes with which it was originally furnished were missing. Instead, some cheap substitutes were there. I asked the policeman who worked with me, "Hamdi Effendi, what happened to the rugs and drapes in this room?" Hamdi said, "Effendi, how many rugs and drapes were in this room?" I said, "Three rugs and four drapes." He said, "Now count them." I said, "The number is the same." "Then," he said, "what are you worried about since the number is the same?" These same officials had settled the matter during the night.

Large sums of money and jewels had been taken from Mr. Leslie's treasury of Armenian valuables and from the Ottoman Bank. The commission seized, also, about 140,000 gold pieces that were kept at the bank as a capital fund. They replaced these with paper money. Of the gold pieces, they returned one because they found it a little too light.

A jeweler from my Assyrian congregation, Mr. Garabed Kouyoumjian, was called to appraise the confiscated jewels. He went every day for one month to do this job. The valuable jewels were then replaced by cheap imitations which were sent to Constantinople.

This commission in one year thus disposed of all the "abandoned" properties of the Armenians in Urfa. Its assignment completed, the members returned home.

23. Turkish Refugees at Urfa

G overnment confiscation of property extended, also, to usable homes left vacant by the decimation of the Armenian population. Here were settled Turkish refugees who had come to Urfa to escape the advancing Russian army in the region of Van and Bitlis. Although they had robbed and killed Armenian refugees encountered on the way, these new arrivals were still hungry and half naked. Whenever they occupied an Armenian home in Urfa, they would gradually tear down the beams and stones and sell them. They would use the rest of the lumber for burning, then move on to another house — even those that were partially destroyed — where they continued the same procedure.

The Turkish government gave the Turkish exiles all the help it could and tried to satisfy all their requests, frequently at the expense of the few surviving Armenians. These efforts brought into sharp focus the negative qualities of the Turkish refugees as contrasted to their Armenian counterparts. I remember especially two instances which clearly illustrate the difference.

In almost every Turkish home in Urfa during the period of deportations there was a captive exiled Armenian woman, girl, or boy. With their cleanliness, reliability, and restraint they found favor with their masters and thus managed to stay alive, at least to have a place to sleep and food to eat. Turkish exiles began to complain, protesting that the local Turks were keeping *giavoors* instead of their own religious and racial sisters and brothers. In order to avoid further discontent, the Turkish government passed a law requiring local Turks to dismiss Armenians in their homes and to take in Turkish refugees in their place. But most of the Turks paid no attention to the directive. A number of them told me personally that the Armenian women and children had been a blessing in their homes, that the Armenian women especially had made their homes much cleaner, more orderly, and more pleasant. They all testified that the Armenians were faithful, never stole. Those who, on order of the government, took Turks into their homes put them out before long because they were dirty and were always stealing.

One morning when I went to work at the government building, Turkish officers were standing outside conversing. I greeted them and joined them.

They were watching passers-by on the road below, among whom were two groups of refugees filing by, one after the other. The first was a group of Turkish refugees — dirty, repulsive, obviously quareling as they scuffled along. Behind them were walking a group of exiled Armenian women and children — quiet, and seemingly solicitous of one another. Turks and Kurds had taken most of their clothes away from them during the march, but as they moved along, the elderly women were spinning yarn by hand, while the younger women were knitting clothes from this wool. (We learned that they had been given the wool by a Turkish *agha* at whose home they had worked during a brief interval.) Lutfi Bey, one of the leaders of the gendarmes watching the sight, was a man educated in Paris. He was so moved by these scenes that, turning to the officials nearby, he exclaimed, "Effendis, look at those two groups! Our people started out taking their possessions with them and received help from the government everywhere, yet they are dirty, miserably clad, and crude. The Armenians, whom we drove out of their homes and repeatedly robbed on the way, are still trying to remain civilized and are even making clothes to wear. Let me make a prophecy: This Armenian nation will never disappear."

24. Famine and Disease

The natural result of destruction and confiscation was a scarcity of everything, especially food. From 1916 through 1918 Urfa was plagued with famine. Many of the local poor and refugees died of starvation. In the evenings at every doorstep could be seen people looking almost like skeletons, whimpering weakly, in Turkish, "*Ahj um . . . Ahj um . . .*" or in Arabic, "*Zhu'an . . . Zhu'an . . .*" or in Armenian, "*Anoti yem . . . Anoti yem . . .* [I am hungry . . . I am hungry.]" It was unbearable. As the night wore on, silence prevailed. Early in the morning when we opened our doors, in front of every house we would see dead from starvation a Turk here, a Kurd there, an Armenian here, an Arab there. Another remembrance of the famine: when the five hundred inmates of the prison in Urfa began chanting, "Ahj um . . . Ahj um . . . ," the whole city resounded with their echo.

The Turkish government did nothing to relieve the famine. It hired "undertakers," dividing them into groups of four. These groups gathered up the Armenian corpses into manure carts and dumped them into ditches outside the city. The Moslem corpses were carried in regular coffins, cleansed and wrapped in white cloth, and buried in their cemeteries. For every Moslem corpse the government gave five yards of burial wrapping cloth and one small cake of soap with which the collectors were expected to prepare the body for interment. In addition, the collectors were each paid five *kurush* (about twenty-five cents) for labor. Each body had to be examined by the coroner before burial. One day the doctor noticed that, although most groups brought a corpse every two or three hours, one group returned every half hour. He became suspicious and put an identifying mark on one corpse brought by that group. He found that this group brought the same body back four times.

Some of the Turks who did have food began to suffer from food poisoning. When the Armenian population was decimated, the city was left without artisans and physicians. Some Turkish families cooked food in unplated bronze pans and were poisoned. The Turkish government, therefore, felt obliged to bring Armenian artisans from Aintab and Berejik, at least partially to fill the needs of the local people. These artisans remained in Urfa as forced laborers. Some died of famine and disease. Some were conscripted into the army in March of 1918 to meet military needs. After the armistice, the survivors returned to their original homes, not knowing that the war was yet to continue in Turkey, and that they would be banished from their Fatherland of twenty-five hundred years.

During the years of famine, the deplorable conditions became worse as various diseases began to spread. The typhus epidemic especially did its destructive work. Every day, in addition to the refugees, from fifty to one hundred townspeople died of typhus alone. Urfa presented a pitiful picture. When famine and typhus began to snatch victims from all classes, it seemed that for a while harassment of the few Armenians here and there was forgotten. Starving Armenians and Turks were begging side by side in front of the same market and together were gathering grass from the fields.

Both as a pastor and as a young citizen I constantly visited people, especially those who were ill, and from time to time I would transfer those who were very ill or helpless to the German hospital. The director, Dr. Kuenzler, and his staff of Armenian nurses willingly helped everyone to the best of their ability.

As was inevitable, within a few weeks I myself contracted typhus and for days lay on my bed unconscious. At the time, Mariam Hanum, the widow of Andon Effendi, and her two daughters were staying at the parsonage. They were among the exiles of Urfa who had been sent to Der-el-Zor after the siege, had survived, and wandered back to the city. I had admitted them into my home until they could get settled, and I had convinced a recalcitrant Turkish official (a friend of her husband) to return her jewels and gold pieces entrusted to him for safekeeping. (Andon Effendi was an Armenian government official in Urfa who had refused to heed my warnings and had been killed during the period of harassment before the siege.) When I became ill, the frightened woman took whatever food was in the house and fled with her daughters. I will be forever grateful to brother Hagop Besos, who discovered me in my condition, visited me regularly, and helped in any way he could for recovery. (His son Vasil, who had invited me to serve their church, had been drafted into the army. Alas! He never returned.) I am indebted, also, to Dr. Kuenzler who gave medical care and to sister Khatun Jamgoch of my congregation for all her help. (She was the wife of one of the Assyrians who had been spared at the ambush of Sheytan Deresi.)

Famine and disease continued. The war was intensifying. Now Turkish youths were being conscripted. *Bedel* was no longer an option. This new ruling was a gold mine for Turkish military officers. Hundreds of Turks obtained draft deferment for their sons by bribing these officials. Many who did not have the money for bribes and were conscripted, then deserted from the army and came to town. Arab and Kurdish villagers found a source of income in robbing these escaped soldiers. The inhabitants would invite the soldiers to their homes, lodge and feed them overnight. Then, after setting them on the road, the hosts would go after the departed guests and rob them of whatever they had. (Robbing a guest in the home was forbidden under their religious laws.) On a few occasions these hosts had quarrels among themselves. They then agreed that each host would rob only his own guest. They abode by this rule and continued this project until the very end.

25. Marie

O ne of the survivors of the battle of Urfa was Marie Hovagimian, who later became my wife. She was not a native of Urfa but an exile from the city of Mezire, the seat of government of the *vilayet* of Harput in central Turkey. (Mezire was on a plain three miles south of the city of Harput, which was a fortress on a hill.) Marie's personal experiences as a refugee had been typical of the more fortunate of the deportees, although, as with all Armenians in those days, tragedy had been an ever-present reality in and around her family.

Marie's paternal grandfather, Simeon, owned several farms in and around Kessirig (another town near Harput) — two wheat, one vegetable, one lumber farm, and three vineyards. During the Massacre of 1895 his wife Varter suggested he hide to avoid being killed. He refused, saying, "It's a sin to kill; they wouldn't do that." He was shortly beheaded. His son, Asadur, Marie's father, did hide and survived the massacre but one month later was beaten to death by the Turks when he tried to help a cousin they were beating at the village military post. Marie was nine months old at the time, and her brother Hagop was seven years old. Asadur was the last surviving child of eleven. Several months later Varter died of grief.

Marie's maternal grandfather, Eleazar Tatevosian, a merchant, died of pneumonia when his daughter Hripsime, Marie's mother, was nine months old. Two years later his wife Anna (Hripsime's mother) married Sarkis Nanian. Hripsime's paternal grandmother would not give up the grandchild until after six more years, when Anna took her daughter home. Four years after that, in 1876, Hripsime was married to Asadur (at the age of thirteen).

After her father-in-law Simeon and her husband Asadur were killed in 1895, Hripsime and her mother-in-law Varter managed the Hovagimian farms. In a few months, when Varter died, Hripsime had to manage them alone. To avoid the advances of local Turks, she moved to the nearby city of Mezire and married a childless widower, Toros Kabayan, who had very little property of his own, was retired, and was content to have his wife run her farms. She traveled daily, on foot, one hour each way. After four years she kept only two of the farms and gave out five of them to tenant farmers, taking a percentage of the profits. Her second husband died suddenly in 1905.

In 1908 Marie's brother Hagop left for America. One of the common dangers for handsome young Armenian boys in those days was attacks by Turkish homosexuals. Armenians had no legal redress, and if they tried to defend themselves against molesters, they were sure to be killed. Hagop found himself increasingly the object of advances by Turkish men. He decided to avoid a fatal confrontation by leaving the country. He planned to return later and build a home on one of the family farms. The outbreak of World War I changed that plan.

Marie lived with her mother in Mezire. She attended first the Protestant elementary school. Then, when that was merged with the German missionary school, she would have had to pass by the Turkish armory en route. She, therefore, transferred to the Apostolic school closer by. After graduation from secondary school in 1912, she taught for three years, until the war came to Mezire.

In June of 1915 all the Armenian town leaders were gathered without explanation into the central government building and detained there. Among these was Nishan Gumushian, a brother-in-law of Hripsime, the husband of one of her three half-sisters. A prominent farmer, he used to supply vegetables and dairy products to the Turkish military. Two or three weeks after being imprisoned, he was allowed to visit his family. Accompanied by guards, he was not allowed to speak, and appeared dazed. Furtively he showed evidences of his tortures. Hot, boiled eggs had been tied to the bottoms of his feet and under his arms. His nails had been pulled out. Within one month after the men were gathered into the armory, the building was empty, and the men were heard from no more.

Early in July the town crier announced that within one week everyone should be ready to leave for Aleppo. No one could ask questions. Marie and Hripsime were in the first of three contingents of about two thousand each to be moved out. Gendarmes accompanied the group as guides and guards. The government gave each household one donkey. Marie and Hripsime bought a second donkey. Thus they could both ride, and they were able to load a generous supply of food, bedding, and many pieces of Marie's handwork. Marie was wearing white gloves and a white hood, and was carrying a parasol as they started out. The activities of the gendarmes soon frightened her into changing her garb. It became obvious that this was not an occasion to travel in style.

The real nature of the journey began to be revealed the second night of the trip, just outside Malatia. At this encampment all males twelve years old and up were separated from the crowd. About five hundred men were gathered in about two hours. The rest of the "pilgrims" were taken to the khan in town. Shortly after midnight the sound of machine guns announced the fate of the men. The following morning those in the *khan* were ordered to leave everything behind and to proceed to another khan. Several hours later they were returned to the first place to find most of their possessions gone. All of Marie's handwork, representing years of irreplaceable work, had been removed.

Traditionally Armenian girls, as soon as they were able to hold a needle, learned the fine art of sophisticated needlework. Those who did well at it devoted countless hours to designing and creating many exquisite pieces. Some they gave as gifts and others they used. Most they kept for their dowries. Over the years Marie had painstakingly labored, often by moonlight, and skilfully produced these unique pieces. They were the most valuable goods she owned. More than that, they were a part of her. She could not leave them behind when she left home. She wept bitterly at the loss. Hripsime could not quiet her. Marie did not recover from this state of shock until Anna Varzhuhi (Teacher Anna), who had left Mezire with the caravan and was with them now in the khan, gave her a therapeutic slap in the face and reminded her, "Marie, my dear, be thankful that all you have lost is your handwork. Don't you see all around you people are losing their honor and their very lives!" Regaining her composure, resigned to her loss, Marie prayed for forgiveness and strength, and tried to avoid thinking about it as they moved on into the wilderness and the uncertain future.

There were more pressing problems to think about. Rape, for instance, and how to avoid it; to plan ways to avoid arousing the Turks' interest. Marie and her mother turned their garments inside out. From the supplies they still carried with them, they sewed patches of rags they tore from other clothes onto these to make them look tattered. Marie made a paste from a little flour from their food bag, and they put the mixture on their skin to look like sores. Marie also simulated a limp, being careful not to change legs. In short, she tried to look as repulsive as possible. Whenever gendarmes made their periodic searches for attractive girls to carry off, Marie took added precautions to escape detection. She hid within her *heybeh* (double-bagged drop cloth or rug to be thrown over the mule). Her head inside the bag at one end and feet inside the bag at the opposite end, she stayed motionless on the ground, surrounded by other paraphernalia, until the danger passed.

Marie and Hripsime were very lucky. They escaped the fate of many of the women. The soldiers frequently frisked the women for things to rob, even probing into the vagina for possible hidden money and jewelry. They tortured and killed whenever they pleased. Many exiles — "pilgrims" was hardly the appropriate word now — died from illness, heat prostration, and fatigue. Corpses were constantly underfoot, as burials were not permitted. Once Marie's donkey stumbled on a corpse and was so frightened that Marie had to get off and lead the animal away before it would proceed again on its own.

After days of wandering — there was no way to know how many — the diminishing caravan reached the shores of the Euphrates, where they encamped to wait for ferries. Here the soldiers entertained themselves by throwing dignified old ladies and suckling babies into the river, and by raping and mutilating more young girls and playfully throwing them into the current. Some of the women threw themselves into the river to avoid indignities.

Before the caravan crossed the Euphrates on rafts, the donkeys were taken away. The rest of the journey continued on foot. Supplies which could not be carried by hand had to be left behind. The soldiers continued their atrocities. In addition, frequently *chettehs* (guerrillas) and Kurds swooped across the rocky wastes to attack the procession. They robbed, raped, and killed in wild orgies. Chettehs were thieves and murderers set free from prisons. These bandits and the Kurds were encouraged by the government to loot, plunder, and kill the *giavoors* at will.

The journey from Mezire southward to Urfa took about two months, during the heat of July and August. Here the survivors — about two hundred out of the original two thousand — were taken to the khan, as a stopover before continuing on to Aleppo. (Some avoided the khan and escaped into the city.) In about ten days, the living deportees — now about forty in number — were directed to transfer to the Apostolic church. By now their coming fate was obvious. Marie and Hripsime, therefore, slipped away and sought refuge at a home across the street from the church, where they stayed for two weeks.

One day about a week after their arrival, Marie was asked to deliver a basket of okra to the Ketenjian home, next door to the home of Mgrdich Yotneghparian. She was surprised at the weight of the basket and on the way looked under the cover to see what was making the bundle so heavy. She noticed that beneath the okra, at the bottom of the basket, were some other wrapped items, though she could not be sure what these were. Marie noticed also, as she walked those few blocks, that two young men (who had been at her host's home) were following her at a distance, behaving much like bodyguards. She hurried along and delivered the basket. Mr. Ketenjian brushed the okra aside and, removing the items at the bottom, was most pleased at receiving the contents. They were bullets. It was now days before the Battle of Urfa. Within a few days Marie and Hripsime were transferred to the Ketenjian home for greater safety.

Late in the morning of September 29, Marie and her friend Zaruhi (another refugee who was staying at Ketenjian's) went to the home of Reverend Akkelian, across the courtyard from the American consulate. They gave him letters for their brothers in America. The Reverend would give these letters to Mr. Leslie, who would then send them on. The girls were at the Akkelian home when the first volleys of the defense of Urfa were heard. They could not leave the pastor's home. The following day he took them, together with his sister Victoria, across the courtyard to the greater security of the consulate. By October 9, word was received that the whole missionary complex had to be evacuated for use as a defense position. By then the Ketenjian residence was also threatened. So both Marie and Hripsime and their companions were once again moved, this time across the street from the consulate to the Hagopjan Yordoghlian residence. Only his wife and youngest son Joseph remained there. Also, a group of young people of Urfa had found refuge there for the duration of the battle. The transferred refugees remained with them. Whenever the fighting intensified, they went down to an underground room available there.

Near the end of the third week of fighting, when the situation seemed hopeless, the young people wanted to escape. Marie refused to join them in spite of her mother's encouragement, not wanting to leave Hripsime behind. As it turned out, before the youths could reach safety, barking dogs led to their discovery. Several young people were shot and killed; only two returned. Joseph Yordoghlian was among those killed.

After the battle, Marie and her mother, like the rest of the surviving refugees brought to Urfa from other cities, were spared immediate harsh treatment, as they had not been "rebels." Plans to drive them into the desert of Der-el-Zor remained unchanged, however. All the refugees were returned to the khan before deportation. Within three days Dr. Kuenzler sent one of his nurses to select a deportee to be taken to his home. She selected Marie, and when Marie refused to be separated from her mother, the nurse took them both. They were first directed to the hospital for physical examinations. Having passed these satisfactorily, they were escorted to the Kuenzler home. They should have considered themselves fortunate, since this meant they would be spared exile into the desert. They were very upset, however, when Mrs. Kuenzler announced her plans to send Marie to the home of a wealthy Turk where she would be "rescued from a life of exile and lead a life of comfort." Marie and Hripsime knew what such a rescue really meant: slavery in a harem. Marie refused to go. That wealthy Turk happened to be Mahmud Nedim, the one who participated in the killing of Zohrab and Vartkes, who rejoiced at the burning of the Armenian quarter and soon afterward became blind.

Marie and her mother were then taken to work at the home of Herr Eckart, who needed household help. He was cruel and demanding, but at least Marie's honor remained safeguarded; mother and daughter were out of danger as long as Eckart needed them. Marie helped with the housework and care of the six children aged six to fifteen years: Edna (the oldest), Martin, Elizabeth, Heine, Gretlein, and Dorothy. Hripsime baked bread in a large basement of a nearby two-story structure in the process of being built. This appeared to be just another house, but later examination showed that it must have been intended as a fort. The size and structure of the building, and the round apertures which could be nothing but gun ports, were evidence. The building was never completed. When Germany lost the war, construction stopped. Upstairs in this unfinished structure were hundreds of rolls of yard goods taken from Armenian merchants, and many dowries of Armenian girls.

Within two days of their arrival at Eckart's, Marie and Hripsime were sought out by Turkish soldiers and returned to the khan, in spite of the German's efforts to keep them. The government was searching every home for Armenian survivors to drive them to Der-el-Zor. Shortly afterward Marie came down with typhus. The epidemic had started, and many at the khan became infected. Soon after Marie recovered, Hripsime fell victim to the disease. She had barely recovered when Herr Eckart's messenger came once more and took Marie and her mother back to his home, where they remained until our marriage. Eckart had convinced the authorities to do him this favor.

Although her assignments were very heavy, Marie was a willing and efficient worker. Mrs. Eckart was very pleased and, therefore, was very cordial to her and at times even solicitous. But the most trying moments for Marie were those occasions when she helplessly witnessed Herr Eckart's cruelty to other Armenians.

On one occasion, when Eckart turned away a widow who had survived the massacres and returned to claim her property entrusted to him, Marie heard him disdainfully say, "You Armenians, your life is not even your own; how can you say 'my money, my wheat'?" and saw him chase the poor woman away. When Marie began weeping at this heartlessness, Mrs. Eckart's words were no consolation whatsoever: "Marie, don't you cry; we are going to take you to Germany." Marie could not hide her distress and continued to weep.

Another time, a boy who had been in the German orphanage, who had survived the massacres and exile and returned to Urfa in a hungry and pitiful state, went to the missionary's home thinking that Eckart would be glad to accept him. "Father, I survived! But I'm hungry and I don't have any place to go. I'll do any work you want done for you. Will you please let me stay here?" Eckart pushed the orphan boy out, growling, "I am the father of Martin and Heine; I am not the father of Armenian dogs like you. Get lost! Go wherever you want!" This was the missionary Eckart who had family prayers every night.

Incidents such as these occurred frequently. In addition, Marie and Hripsime witnessed that disturbing transaction daily when the Turk Ahmed Agha delivered to Eckart at his home the money for the stolen Armenian goods sold locally, and received his share.

26. Someone to Weep for Me

When I first came to Urfa, I had no plans for marriage. I intended to return to Marash before taking that step. But when I recovered from typhus, the words of the writer Bedros Tourian came to me: "One who is about to die wants two things: first life, and then, someone to weep for him." I decided I wanted someone to weep for me. Previously when friends had suggested marriage to me, I had said, "That's for Germans and Turks these days, not for Armenians." Dr. Kuenzler was one of those friends. I told him now about my change of outlook and asked him to introduce me to the girl he had in mind. I made the same request of Varter, a member of my congregation. She was an exile from Mezire. Her father and husband had been killed just before the deportations. Her seventh child had been born early in the march and had died immediately. Two of her children and her husband's parents were killed during the march. (Her mother, who was exiled with another group, reached Aleppo, but died before Varter could see her.) One morning Varter awoke to find the caravan departed and out of sight. Alone in the desert with her remaining four children aged two to eight, she sought refuge in a dry well.

An Arab, searching for hideaways, discovered Varter and her children, and threatened to throw rocks into the well if they did not come out. He insisted that the mother come out first, and, repeating his threat, rejected any alternative, but promised to get the children out after the mother. He then broke his promise and refused to get the children out. He dragged Varter away while the children cried after her. (Their crying voices — Mamma, Mamma — haunted her the rest of her life.) The Arab later sold her to a Turkish gendarme who brought her to Urfa, set her up in a separate apartment in order to spare her the strain of being with another wife, and tried to please her in any way possible, short of giving her freedom. When she asked him for a Bible, he came to me. I gave a Bible and a hymnal for which she was very grateful. He told me he was moved by her singing, and when I suggested he bring her to church, he agreed to drop her off at my study and pick her up from there every Sunday, to make it possible for her to attend services without his being in jeopardy. My study was in the church school building, next to my living quarters. (Soon after my recovery from typhus I had to give up the parsonage for soldiers to be quartered there for several months.)

Varter told me that she had heard that a former neighbor of hers from Mezire was at Herr Eckart's home. She promised to get more information, as she thought we were well suited to each other. One Sunday after church, when I went to my study, I found a young lady present with Varter. She was introduced as Marie Hovagimian. With her was Edna Eckart.

About three months after the end of the battle, when the city seemed to be settling down, Marie had asked Eckart permission to go to church. He had agreed on condition that the oldest daughter Edna accompany Marie. Since the Armenian churches were still unopened and ours was the only church functioning then, they came there. It was on the first Sunday that they appeared that Varter brought the girls to my study to chat and thereby, also, to introduce Marie and me. During our first conversation Marie sought help for a former teaching colleague of hers, Rebecca Santourjian, who had been taken to the home of an Arab pasha. I investigated with the help of a gendarme who, sad to say, brought word that she had died of typhus.

The girl that Dr. Kuenzler had in mind for me turned out to be Marie Hovagimian, also. A third friend had made the same suggestion. After having seen Marie, I tended to agree with my friends. Dr. Kuenzler arranged for me to visit her at Eckart's home, and there in the garden I told her of my intentions. Her first reaction was, "How can an Armenian think about marriage in 1916?" I answered, "If we stay apart, we are in greater danger of dying. Together we can help each other. If we die, let's die together." She still hesitated: "I have a brother in America. I want to go there to be near him before I marry." I promised to take her and her mother to America after getting married. Finally, she commented, "But we don't know each other." Through eight months of correspondence we became well enough acquainted. Two of Marie's former neighbors delivered these letters. They were among the refugees who had been placed in Assyrian homes after the battle, as Marie and her mother were placed with the Eckarts. We are indebted to Nouritsa Kazanjian and Maritsa Zhamakordzian who walked an hour for each delivery but were happy to be of help.

When I told Herr Eckart of our decision to be married, he was furious. He raged, "We are destroying Armenian families. Do you intend to start an Armenian family before my very eyes? I am going to have you hanged tomorrow!" I retorted, "Herr Eckart, I'll have you hanged tomorrow morning; then in the afternoon I'll get hanged." Eckart was shocked: "How will you do that?" I elucidated, "The abandoned goods of the Armenians belong to our government [Turkish], not to you. But you have filled your warehouses with the dowries of Armenian girls and the treasures of the Armenian people." He understood and became frightened: "Why are you upset? I was just fooling. Why would I have you hanged? You're a faithful worker in the government office." He soothed, "You and Marie are both Armenian. You belong to each other. There's no denying it." He agreed to release Marie whenever I might notify him. I suppose he could have killed me anyway, but I think he was too afraid of the possible consequences, knowing that Dr. Kuenzler and the government officials were my supporters.

The American Dr. John Merrill was in town at the time, among other things to investigate the death of Mr. Leslie. (He had to accept the official explanation.) He was the only ordained minister available to perform the marriage ceremony. Although Dr. Kuenzler was authorized to perform weddings legally, he was not a minister. I suggested to Marie, "Let's get married while Dr. Merrill is here to administer the vows." She agreed.

Immediately after I had left Eckart, he had growled at Hripsime, "You have increased your age and decreased your brains. How can you let your daughter marry that man?" She had answered, "He's a fine Christian." The next day Hripsime quietly left the Eckart household and went to the Assyrian home where Maritsa Zhamakordzian and Nouritsa Kazanjian were staying.

Three days later I sent word for Marie to leave her work. Eckart had expected to take her to Germany as a permanent member of the household staff. He hated to give her up. He had had a heated argument with Dr. Kuenzler the day after my original disclosure of our intentions, blaming the doctor for having arranged the match. Nevertheless, Marie was able to leave and to join her mother. Hripsime had saved three gold pieces for any emergency. Marie used some of that money now to buy material for a wedding gown. She found suitable fabric in town, sewed the gown, and was ready in a week.

On October 18, 1916, in the presence of Marie's friends and about seven or eight deacons and several others from my congregation, we were married in the parsonage, where I had once again moved in. The service was conducted in Turkish. Dr. Merrill did not know Armenian. In fact, all church services were conducted in Turkish, as the use of the Armenian language in church was prohibited at this time. Marie did not understand any Turkish, but she soon learned.

27. Armistice

A fter the Battle of Urfa the Armenian quarter remained desolate and in ruins. Disease and famine continued to plague the city for another three years. Marie and I worked together after our marriage, both among our Assyrian congregation and on behalf of the many refugees. I continued my work as interpreter at the Turkish government offices, particularly in the task of the disposition of Armenian properties, about which I have already written. This work, with all its risks, provided an unexpected blessing. Ismael Bey paid for my services with grain, which was much more valuable than money during the existing famine. This kept not only our own family but also a number of others, with whom we shared the grain, from starvation.

Two new sources of help came for our work with the townspeople and refugees. An Armenian major, Dr. Yervant Bey, the personal physician of Ali Ihsan Pasha, the chief of the Turkish army at Bagdad, stayed at Urfa for a while. He graciously treated many Armenian and Assyrian patients. He was allowed to help, since persecution was relaxed after the battle.

The other source of help was a group of German soldiers who sometimes came from Aleppo on freight convoys hauling grain. They were for the most part clean cut, well mannered, conscientious young men. Through the intercession of Dr. Kuenzler we were able to rescue a number of Armenian girls and women from the Turks and send them to freedom to Aleppo with these soldiers on their return trip. Varter was among these. She found her way to America and remarried.

These German soldiers were a welcome contrast to the ruthless Herr Eckart. We met one other German whose cruelty matched Eckart's. He was a military officer who came from Aleppo en route to Mosul, accompanied by a Turkish lieutenant and an Assyrian workman who told the following story. A short while earlier some Armenian deportees had passed by, alongside the road on which these men were traveling. Many of the exiles had fallen on the way and died from fatigue and hunger. Leaning on the lifeless body of a young mother in this group, a small child of about two years was crying, "Mommy . . . Mommy . . . ." The Turkish lieutenant, pitying the child, had the car stopped, picked up the little boy, and started to wipe his tears. The German officer, turning to the Turk, angrily snapped,

"Isn't that infant the child of an Armenian? We do not want a single Armenian to be left alive. How can you, against your government's orders, want to save an Armenian child?" So saying, he grabbed the little boy by the feet, flung him to the side of the road, and ordered the driver to start the car up again. Ironically, it was the Turk who said, "You ungodly, brutal scoundrel! How can you not pity this poor, innocent child?"

For the duration of the war, Urfa was one of the Turkish military training centers from which soldiers were sent to the Mesopotamian front and the Caucasus. The chief of training was a German, Major Bilel, who had as his assistant a German captain. Officers of the Turkish army served under them, and among those assigned here in 1916 and 1917 were Kapriel Noradungian (Major Bilel's interpreter), Kalust Aijian, Sisak Tateosian, and several other Armenians. They were among the fortunate few who had been spared the fate of the majority of the Armenian soldiers and who had been allowed to remain alive. (To satisfy the needs of the army, the government spared a few essential professionals and tradesmen — doctors, pharmacists, tailors, shoemakers, carpenters, pewterers, etc.) In fact, all were well treated by both Turkish and German officers and were allowed to move about freely during off-duty hours. They often visited our home, where we exchanged information and gave each other encouragement.

By the fall of 1918 news of the surrender and retreat of German and Turkish troops was reaching us, and the Turks seemed daily to grow more discouraged. Especially frightening for the Turks was the advance of General Edmund Allenby's British troops toward Jerusalem, Damascus, and Aleppo. On October 30, 1918, the Armistice of Mudros was signed by Turkey and Great Britain, and on November 11 came the general armistice which ended the war. The Turkish people were sad over their defeat but were happy that this curse called war was over. As for the poor and hungry folk, they seemed to gain new strength through their joy, and poured into the markets. The price of bread suddenly dropped from twenty-five to two *kurush* (ten cents), and a few well-to-do Turks, as an act of charity, bought up loaves of bread from the bakers and gave them out to the poor. These pitiful souls took the fresh, white bread in their hands, so overjoyed and excited that they could not eat, just gazed at the bread and smiled, then kissed the bread and each other.

When the Turkish officials of Urfa heard news of their defeat and of the armistice, they were apprehensive. They began to put the blame for the Armenian massacres on the Ittihad Party and to condemn them for having been responsible for dragging Turkey into the war, for trying to annihilate the Armenian nation, and for destroying the land. Several of the higher officials solicited my friendship, and some even showed a willingness to accept Christianity. When Armenian survivors who had returned to Urfa would walk through the markets, their Turkish neighbors expressed delight at seeing them alive and back. The new *mutesarif*, Ali Rizza Bey, called me and stated that he was ready to help the returning Armenians in any way he could.

Most of the returnees were women and children — refugees who had been living in Arab and Kurdish homes in towns around Urfa. As soon as they heard of the armistice, they escaped one by one into Urfa.

Every Armenian who returned to Urfa and stepped into the Armenian quarter, forgetting personal problems, could not withhold tears upon seeing everything in ruins, with the bones of beloved martyrs strewn here and there. Nevertheless, putting their thoughts to the future, they were happy to find some survivors and eager to rebuild.

At this time Dr. Kuenzler asked us to devote all our time to the rehabilitation of the returning refugees. To make this possible, he found a new pastor for the Assyrian congregation. We received permission from the Turkish government to make arrangements for the returning exiles. The women were placed at the St. Sarkis Monastery outside of town. For the boys and girls we started an orphanage in the American mission buildings. Marie and I took care of both groups until the arrival of the officers of the Near East Relief at Urfa. With a group of assistants we worked day and night to feed, clothe, and rehabilitate them, to restore the Armenian Christian faith and character in them. In a short time their number reached one thousand, and soon afterward, fifteen hundred. We immediately started sewing and weaving groups for the women. Together with help from some townspeople, these women sewed new clothes and made new quilts and bedding for all the children. With careful planning, Marie saw to it that three meals a day were served with the money that was allotted for two.

Discipline might have been a problem for these children who had become used to a primitive life style among the Moslem villagers for the last three years. But they liked their new quarters and responded quickly to the love and care shown them. To accomplish the more difficult task of helping them to relearn their native Armenian language and Christian precepts, we organized a school, where every morning I conducted worship services and taught them Armenian prayers and hymns.

One of the problems we faced was the danger of losing some of our charges. A number of women and girls who had come from the homes of wealthy Moslems wanted to return to the greater physical comforts they enjoyed there. Sometimes it became more difficult to convince them to stay. They had lost their self-respect within the security offered by slavery, uncertain as that security was. In most cases we were successful in reawakening the desire to be self-reliant and to develop their individual potential. Sometimes Turks or Arabs or Kurds would come at night to steal back the boys and girls who had come from their homes. Dr. Kuenzler and I asked the chief of police to place guards outside the buildings. Police were placed as guards, but often they were not interested in preventing the kidnapping. I, therefore, personally spent many long hours standing as armed guard during the nights.

On the whole, our efforts toward rehabilitation were productive. When the Americans of the Near East Relief visited our operations, they were so attracted to our little factory, where the women were sewing and weaving, that they took pictures of it which they published in papers and books in the United States. When they visited the morning service, they were amazed that these children, most of whom had come so recently from the wilderness, could sing without a mistake the intricate, long form of the Armenian Doxology.

28. A Reluctant Mission to Aleppo

One day early in January, 1919, a British armored car came into Urfa. In it were a captain (Captain Sharkey) and two soldiers. They went directly to the home of Dr. Kuenzler. In the evening the captain called me for a conference and made a special request: "According to the general terms of the armistice, the British army has no right to occupy Urfa; but one section of that treaty gives us that right if the people of Urfa ask for our protection. We have, therefore, come on behalf of the British commander at Aleppo to invite you to come there to present such a petition to Sir Mark Sykes. He is the British representative in this region."

From the flimsy pretext to be used for the occupation, it was obvious to me that the "protection" would be temporary and that the aftermath might be catastrophic if the Turks were to get the upper hand again. I declined the captain's invitation, explaining to him, "First of all, I am not a political official and do not wish to become involved in a political matter. Secondly, I suspect that after being here for a short time, you will withdraw. Then our position will be even worse than before, and we may be subjected to another massacre." Captain Sharkey did not like my answer, but he kept his composure and tried to convince me that my going would most certainly be helpful to the surviving Armenians and Assyrians of Urfa. (There were five thousand Assyrians in Urfa at that time, and probably a like number of Armenians, including exiles from Urfa who had returned, exiles from elsewhere who had remained in Urfa, and the more than one thousand orphans at the orphanage.) Captain Sharkey maintained that if I refused to go, most likely the remaining Christians would be killed, and I would be responsible. I remained unconvinced by the captain's words and stood firm on my refusal. In fact, his statement indicated to me that the Allied victory held no guarantee of security for us. But when the Armenians in town heard of the invitation, they demanded that I go to Aleppo. No one seemed to share my concern that agreeing to this British plan might put our Christian community in greater jeopardy with the Turks after the predictable British withdrawal. They rejected the suggestion that artificial restraints imposed on our behalf by an Allied power, once withdrawn, could unleash harsh, retaliatory measures. Thus, although still uneasy about the consequences to myself, my family, and the community, I went to Aleppo. As a precaution, I did not leave with Captain Sharkey. To avoid an obvious relationship between my trip and his return, I waited until a few days after he had returned to Aleppo.

When I presented myself to Sir Mark Sykes, the British representative, he gave me an extraordinarily cordial reception. He was very pleased to receive the required petition and asked also for data on current conditions in Urfa. He sent the papers to General Allenby who then issued orders to occupy Urfa.

Sir Mark Sykes asked me to go also to the British Intelligence Office before leaving Aleppo, to give information on the Armenian massacres at Urfa, including names of those responsible. He promised to keep the information confidential and to withhold my name. The following day, while I was telling of the atrocities committed against the Armenians by the Ittihad Party leaders — Mahmud Nedim, Sheikh Saffad, and Shakir Bey — a phone call from Kilis announced that the same Shakir Bey (of Urfa) had arrived there from Constantinople and was returning to Urfa. The question was directed to Captain Sharkey: "Shall we let him go or shall we arrest him?" The captain ordered Shakir Bey to be arrested and sent to Aleppo.

There was a great deal of unrest in Aleppo. The Germans had left except for a few officers and their families. The German hospital had been closed down. The Turks did not like the British, who had come in. While I was in Aleppo, a riot broke out by Turks and Arabs. I had dropped in at my Uncle Astor's home one day. (They had moved to Aleppo in 1905 when harassment by the tax collector made Marash intolerable.) Mother Shamlian had asked me to escort the two younger daughters home from school to assure their safety. Just after I had brought them home and was about to leave, shooting began in the streets. Prison doors had been thrown open, and all the prisoners, criminal as well as political, were released. The riot lasted several hours before running its course.

As soon as the riot in Aleppo was over, in mid-March, I hastened to return to Urfa before the entry of the British troops, again to neutralize any suspicions the Turkish officials might have regarding my trip to Aleppo. They accepted the fact that I had been on a mission to bring clothes and bedding for the orphans (which I did bring). On Sunday I had special services for the orphans and for the people of the Armenian quarter. I urged them to be cautious in their behavior among the Turks, even after the British occupation, always keeping in mind that those troops might withdraw at any time. I advised the men to continue to wear fezzes, not hats, in deference to the internal administration.

My safe return to Urfa was doubly joyous, since the week before my arrival home our first child, daughter Alice, was born. After so many losses in the family, an addition was especially welcome.

Within a few days the British army entered Urfa. The following day the commander of the troops, Major Burrows, came to our home and took me with him as an interpreter on a visit to the *mutesarif*, Ali Rizza Bey. The mutesarif greeted us very fearfully. Major Burrows spoke to him cautiously and discreetly: "You know, of course, Sir, that you have been defeated and that I have been sent by the British government to assume full authority. You will remain at your post, so also all the other officials. If I see that you govern with justice, and that you protect the rights of all citizens, especially Christians, I will be simply your helpful guest. But if I see that you show injustice toward Christians, I have the authority to dismiss you and to take over the reins of government myself. Therefore, your performance will determine my performance."

Stunned by this unexpected leniency and friendly words, the mutesarif thanked the major over and over again, and promised to rule equitably and to help any Armenians who might appeal for aid.

After leaving the office, Major Burrows accompanied me to my home and visited with Mrs. Jernazian and me. He confirmed my expectations: "Reverend, please tell your congregation to live carefully with the Turks, knowing that we will eventually withdraw from the city and that you will again be subjects of the Turkish government."

This position of the British irritated some of the Armenians. Why did the British come at all if they had no long-term plans to assure security in the region? What game were they playing this time? But most were happy that Major Burrows had at least revealed the truth frankly and cautioned us. On the whole, during the nine months of British occupation safety prevailed everywhere, and we had a peaceful interlude. Armenians returning from exile began to rebuild their demolished homes and make them liveable again, still optimistic that the peace settlement would give them the rights they were so long denied in their homeland.

The American Near East Relief Committee arrived right after the British occupation of Urfa. Marie and I worked together with them for a while to help make a smooth transition, finally leaving the orphanage and monastery totally in their hands. We then accepted the pastorate of the Armenian Evangelical Church at Urfa, since a sizeable congregation had returned, permission to re-open had been given, and they needed a minister.

At this time Kemal's forces were taking over Turkey. Mustafa Kemal Pasha was the leader of a new Turkish resistance which refused to accept the capitulation after the armistice. He and his followers succeeded the discredited and dissolved Ittihad Party in power, pointedly ignored orders of the sultan, established a new capital at Ankara, and eventually drove the sultan out. They launched a nationalistic revolution, gaining support from the European powers by playing them against each other through offering separate economic and political concessions. It later became evident that the oil fields of Mosul had won the British over to their cause. Like the Young Turks before him, while professing democracy and calling his government a republic, Kemal ruled as an autocratic dictator. He promoted an even more determined attack on the non-Turkish citizens of the country. As for the Armenians, he made sure that all efforts of survivors to rebuild their homes and communities were crushed and that any remnants from his new massacres had no choice but to leave the country or become Turkified.

Signs of danger appeared again in Urfa within a few weeks after the British entry. Shakir Bey was set free to return to Urfa, even though anti-British documents had been found in his possession. When I confronted Captain Sharkey (who was now back in Urfa) with the protest, "Why did you arrest him, and why have you now set him free?" the captain, after a lengthy discussion, finally revealed the new British stance: "Poor Reverend, do you think the British government is going to jeopardize relations with the Turkish government just for the sake of a handful of Armenians?" Unable to conceal my chagrin and anger, I retorted, "I have always been aware of this heartless diplomacy of you British, but I had to hear it from you directly."

Rev. Aram Bagdikian, while in Constantinople, had an experience similar to mine concerning the duplicity of British diplomacy. Shortly after the armistice, during the British and French occupation of the city, when Reverend Bagdikian went to British headquarters, above the entrance was written, "Turks are not admitted." A few weeks later when he went again, at the same entrance was written, "Armenians are not admitted." The British had reversed their position and were now fraternizing with the Turks.

Although the British on the one hand sometimes helped Armenians financially, on the other hand, instead of disarming the Turks as the terms of the armistice stated, they armed them further to fight against the French. The French, of course, were not asleep. They had their spies who watched and reported every move the British made. For us Armenians, the situation was becoming discouraging. Enthusiasm in rebuilding was waning as dark clouds of hopelessness were spreading over us. It had finally become clear that all the promises made to the Armenians by the Allied Powers during the war were forgotten, and the Armenians were once again sacrificed in the foul game of European competition for political and economic gains.

The French at last demanded that the British withdraw from Cilicia and Syria, according to the terms of the armistice. The British were anticipating this demand and were ready to evacuate. They had already, during their temporary occupation, accomplished their aims. They had made agreements with the Turks and incited them against the French.

By November, 1919, the British relinquished Cilicia and Syria to the French. What I had suspected and Major Burrows had confirmed became a reality. The British withdrew from Urfa. Before leaving, Major Burrows paid us one last visit. He offered to move our family to Aleppo with him, in appreciation for my help to him. We thanked him but, of course, refused: "First, please take our people out of Urfa, then us." He was very much moved: "I am sorry that as a military man I must obey my orders; I have to withdraw my troops and leave you to your fate. Yes, after us the French will come; but, as you surmise, there will be new battles and, most likely, new massacres by the Turks. I know that you will be one of the first victims. That is why I want to do you a personal favor." The offer was generous and tempting, but I simply could not leave my people in these circumstances. I answered, "I greatly appreciate your gracious sentiments and invaluable offer, but I am sorry that I cannot leave my people in this condition and go away."

29. Word of Honor

S hortly after the departure of the British soldiers, a French battalion of five hundred infantrymen came to Urfa, without artillery, planes, or wireless equipment. Their presence did not seem reassuring. When the British soldiers, including the Indian troops, had come to Urfa, they had marched grimly through the streets without paying attention to the local people — without looking at them or speaking to them. But when the French came, they chatted and laughed as they walked, and often even tried to lift the veils from the faces of the Turkish women. One day they entered the courtyard of the Great Mosque and began to dance. The Turks were barely able to control their tempers, knowing that they would soon have the opportunity to punish the French as they pleased.

Within a month Namuk Pasha, formerly Ali Saib, chief of gendarmes in Urfa and now a henchman of Mustafa Kemal Pasha, arrived in Urfa with his Nationalist soldiers. The local Turks were already prepared to participate in an uprising. When the French commander, Major Hauger, was informed and warned by the Armenians of the impending revolt, he did not want to listen. On February 9, 1920, the Turks gave the French an ultimatum to leave the city. The French refused. The Turks immediately began to attack under the direction of Namuk Pasha.

When we Armenians saw the plight of Urfa worsening, we took two important steps. First, we made plans to defend our sector. Secondly, we did not join the French, since we did not believe they would defend our interests any more than the British did. The French did not want our participation, anyway. Also, our quarter was adjacent to the Turkish quarter, therefore very precariously situated. Our strength next to that of the Turks was nothing. We could have held out hardly one or two days in case of attack, once again to die honorably. The Turks were glad that we did not join the French. They stopped the attacks they had started on us the first two days of fighting, and against which we had fired back. Soon afterwards the Turks demanded that we give them access to the French through our streets. Of course, we could not agree to that. They, therefore, besieged us and would not allow us to buy food outside of our quarter. Occasionally they fired on us but avoided all-out attack, no doubt waiting to starve us into submission. So, like two threatening Damocletian swords, slaughter and starvation dangled over our heads. We collected food from those who had reserves and shared this with those who had none and so, by the grace of God, we escaped both kinds of death.

Days and weeks passed; the fighting grew heavier, but no help came for the beleaguered French. After a month, a French plane came by and dropped a message to the French soldiers saying, "Be of courage. In a few days help and provisions will reach you." But, alas, neither help nor provisions arrived.

Just before the initial attack by Namuk Pasha, Lobud Bey, one of the Turkish notables of Urfa, had said, "We have bought the French soldiers in Urfa by a transaction with Paris. No help will come to them, and we will kill them." Lobud Bey's statement was verified. Two months passed and no help came. That year we had an unusually severe winter, and some of the French soldiers suffered with frozen feet. Severe winter, famine, an enemy force more than ten times greater than their own — these drove the French to despair. Consequently, Major Hauger negotiated with the Turks, using Armenians as intermediaries, to leave Urfa peacefully.

On April 10, 1920, when Captain Sajous, upon orders from Major Hauger, took down the French flag with tears in his eyes, unable to endure the humiliation, he killed himself. The Turks had gladly accepted the offer of the French and gave their word of honor to give them a clear road to start out toward Jarablus (the ancient Carchemish) across the border. But even as this promise was being made, thousands of Turkish soldiers and guerrillas began taking positions on hills along both sides of the mountainous road, to ambush the French and kill them. Even Turkish women participated by carrying water and food to the guerrillas. Hauger ignored early warnings by the Armenians; he insisted that the Turks had given him their *parole d'honneur* (word of honor). Hauger did not proceed along the roads in the plains of Harran, as suggested by the Armenians, but along the mountainous route through Suruj, and fell directly into the trap set for him and his men. When they reached the ravine called Shebekeh, the Turkish equestrian guides suddenly turned back, and the Turkish soldiers and guerrillas on both sides of the ravine opened fire on the French soldiers. Almost all five hundred of them, including two Armenian youths who had joined them, were slaughtered with every conceivable barbarity. The Turks cut off the heads of Major Hauger and several other officers, mounted them on poles, and paraded them through the streets boasting, "This is the fate of those who oppose Islam."

One of the officials of the American Near East Relief had left with the soldiers. When the massacre started at the Shebekeh ravine, he immediately held up a white handkerchief to attract attention. A Turkish officer saw him and ordered the two soldiers who were about to attack not to kill the American. They did not kill him, but took him prisoner and subjected him to all sorts of indignities before releasing him.

Two French officers managed to hide behind rocks and escape. Wandering among friendly, nomadic Kurds, they were eventually discovered and forced to march back to town. After being treated at the German hospital, they were kept in prison for a time, then transferred, one to Aleppo and one to Diarbakir, and eventually sent home to France.

News reached Urfa — I do not recall the source — that when the two officers started to tell their friends at home about the treacherous ambush by the Turks, the French authorities summoned them before a military tribunal and forbade them to repeat the story. The French government put a strict censorship on the episode. We had to believe this news was true when months later letters came to Urfa from the distraught mothers, wives, and sisters of several of those five hundred French soldiers. They had had no news of their sons, husbands, and brothers for all those months and begged for some information. Since these letters were in French, they were referred to me as official interpreter. Unfortunately, I could not tell them the truth. The censors would never allow the facts to pass. If I tried, I would be prevented from carrying on any further effective work in Urfa. With great difficulty I refrained from answering.

British reaction to the plight of the French in Urfa was as might be expected. It was repeated everywhere that when the British officials in Aleppo heard the five hundred French soldiers had been ambushed and slain, those same officials who had released Shakir Bey and armed the Turks sneered, "Good, the egg we laid in Urfa hatched just the chick we wanted."

One of the prominent Turks of Urfa, Shevket Bey, remarked to me, "Effendi, we killed the Armenians; we got away with it. We killed the French; we got away with it. Why shouldn't we kill?"

While the Turkish soldiers and guerrillas who had killed the French soldiers were parading around town with the heads of the French officers speared on top of poles, shouting out, "This is the fate of those who oppose Islam," the director of American Relief, Miss Mary Caroline Holmes, called me and wanted to know where the sound of guns had been coming from and what the confusion in the Turkish quarter was all about. I explained to her that the Turks had killed the French and were celebrating the event. Miss Holmes was very angry and objected, "That news must be some Armenian gossip. The Turks gave their word of honor that the French would go freely." I answered, "Miss Holmes, just wait. Soon you will see whether that news is Armenian gossip or a base Turkish crime committed before your very eyes." I went home disturbed.

A half hour had hardly passed by when Miss Holmes called me again. When I entered this time, she said, wiping the tears from her eyes, "Reverend, forgive me for not believing you a little while ago. We verified again and again that the news you gave is true. I know now that the Turks are a lying and deceitful people." But she hardly understood my next comment: "Miss Holmes, I know definitely that very soon Turkish officials will come and will attribute those massacres to a band of guerrillas, appear to be innocent of the scheme, adding that they will surely punish the offenders. I predict that you will again believe their lies. That is when I will really be troubled."

I had hardly finished my statement when word came that Mutesarif Ali Rizza Bey and the military commander Namuk Pasha wanted to see me. I met them in the courtyard of our church, which was adjacent to the American buildings. The *mutesarif* said to me, "Vaiz Effendi, will you please gather the people in the church. I have something to say to them." We Armenians were afraid that the Turkish mob in their state of frenzy would suddenly advance upon us with their bloody hands. Suspecting that the mutesarif might be setting us up for a massacre, I requested, "Your Honor, the church sanctuary is filled with sick people and infants. Could you please give your message in the courtyard of our church?" Our young people were maintaining armed watch in the courtyard, and we would have a better chance to defend ourselves, if necessary. He agreed to speak in the courtyard.

Mutesarif Ali Rizza Bey said to the people, "My children, it is enough that, deceived by Europeans, you have been slain. It is a pity; you have no more blood left to spill. Today Allah has given this land to us; therefore, you should obey us. If tomorrow He should take it away from us and give it to you, then we will obey you. Do not be afraid. Go to your homes and everyone carry on your work. We are brothers in a common Fatherland." But he did not mention how many times we had felt the knife and perished in the bosom of that Fatherland.

After he had finished his message, Ali Rizza Bey asked me to present himself and Namuk Pasha to the Americans. At this meeting Miss Holmes, greatly disturbed, questioned the officials: "Gentlemen, after giving the French your word of honor that they would be free to go out safely, why did you cruelly kill them even before they had departed from the city?" With typical Turkish hypocrisy Ali Rizza Bey explained, "My lady, believe me, we did not know anything about it; a group of guerrillas went and killed a few Frenchmen. When we heard about it, we immediately put a stop to it. Be assured that we will punish the guilty ones." Miss Holmes turned to me and said, "Badveli, you see, they didn't know anything about it." I was so angry, I began shaking and with difficulty contained myself.

Namuk Pasha then turned to me saying, "Sir, ask these Americans for me why they have come to our country. If they have brought us Musa [Moses], Isa [Jesus], or even Mohammed, let them go back because both Moses and Jesus as well as Mohammed have come out of our land. We have suffered enough on their account. But if the Americans bring us money, guns, and machines, they are welcome. We will give them a place of honor."

In one brief statement Namuk Pasha had given a prophetic summary of Turkish-American relations for years to come. I am today constantly reminded of it as I observe our ongoing diplomacy in Turkey, especially in the years since the second World War. I cannot help but wonder what St. Paul and the dedicated missionaries after him would say about the work of our contemporary American Board of Foreign Missions that supports schools which forbid the mention of Jesus Christ and teach the gospel of

Mammon and Materialism. What, in fact, would the early founders of the American missions say about today's Board, which joins our politicians and businessmen in defense of those who justify or deny the Genocide and ongoing minority persecution, lest the truth jeopardize business opportunities, covering all beneath the veil of "national security"?

30. Uncertain Fate

After the massacre of the French soldiers on April 10, 1920, we were again left in the hands of the Turks. Finally discouraged about any European occupation, we advised our people — particularly the young people — to leave the city one at a time without attracting attention, since we knew that the Turk would give no rest to the Armenian in Urfa. A slow exit began. But, of course, the bulk of the people had no place to go and no means to move. Thus, resigning ourselves to an uncertain fate, we remained in the city, and each of us worked hard to make a living.

For a time, conditions were tolerable. At this point the Turks were fearful of retaliation for the murder of the French battalion and were therefore lenient towards Christians. Of particular concern to us during this period was the plight of the children who had been brought back to Urfa after having spent four or five years since the deportations among Moslem villagers, usually Kurds or Arabs, occasionally Turks. Their fathers for the most part had been killed. Some of these children had actually been placed by their own mothers with friendly Moslem families at the beginning of exile, with the understanding that the children would be returned to the mothers if they survived, otherwise kept by the villagers. Those mothers who had been fortunate enough to survive had reclaimed their children after the armistice with no difficulty. Some of the children had been kidnapped from their mothers during deportation. Some of these surviving mothers had located their children after a long search. In some cases these villagers had given up the kidnapped children without much fuss. In other cases, they had given them up only after endless pleading by the mothers.

All these widows with their children were trying to make a start again in the Armenian quarter of Urfa. Some found their homes liveable, though damaged. Others found their homes unliveable and managed to find other shelter. They were glad to be back alive. But the children had forgotten how to speak Armenian and remembered nothing about Jesus Christ or about the restraints of civilized society. Unlike the children in the orphanage who responded readily to the structured discipline and rehabilitation there, these children were getting out of control and becoming a problem for their mothers and for the community. They were running around the streets fighting, shouting rough Arabic, Kurdish, or Turkish obscenities, and singing incantations in these same languages.

A personal request from Vartuhi Hanum Kulahian spurred us to action. She had entrusted her property, including a silo of grain, to Herr Eckart at the time of the deportation. She had survived and made her way back to Urfa. When she asked Herr Eckart for some of her grain, he beat her up and drove her away. Her husband had been one of the early victims of arrest and execution. When deportations began, she had left her three small sons in the care of Arab workmen on her wheat fields, believing that this would be the only means of saving their lives. She had recovered the boys after her return from the wilderness, but found that they remembered no Armenian and were very undisciplined. She begged us to do something to educate her sons.

Mrs. Jernazian and I, therefore, launched a new project to help not only Vartuhi's sons but all the other children in the Armenian community. We cleaned up the school building of our Evangelical Church, made minor repairs as we were able, and built benches from scrap wood collected at the rug factory. One Sunday we announced from the pulpit that we had room for forty boys and girls in the new school. The benches were filled immediately. As the number of children increased, we built more benches, and then accommodated more by placing cushions on the floor. We recruited two additional teachers to help us. By the end of one year, the enrollment reached three hundred.

We were able to meet expenses by charging students a small fee and by assuring help through Dr. Kuenzler. Paper was impossible to get. So Marie and her mother gathered pieces of paper (that were clean on one side) strewn about yards and streets, including many segments of house deeds. They cut them to uniform size and stitched them to form notebooks for the children. For pencils, at first we used the charred tips of small sticks gathered from the burnt rubble of Armenian homes. Later, Dr. Kuenzler was able to supply real pencils for the school. We received wholehearted support from our congregation as well as from the Apostolic community. To reflect the broad base, we called it Armenian National School rather than Armenian Evangelical School, and we formed a Board of Trustees of qualified townspeople.

It is with a heavy heart that I must relate that one or two disturbed men, seeing that they were not selected for the Board, reported me to the Turkish government as one who was operating a school without a license. I was summoned to headquarters under escort of two policemen. An official there informed me of the charge against me: "Sir, we have received word that you are operating a school without a permit." I explained to him that we had obtained a permit several years ago but that during the recent events the one who had obtained the document had been killed, and the license itself had been lost. I suggested, "You can find a copy of the permit in your records. And, Your Honor, even if we did not have a license, would it be considered a crime for us to rescue our children from roaming about the streets?" The official answered, "Certainly not! I personally appreciate what you are doing, and I will give you a new permit so that no one will trouble you after this." He ordered the director of education to visit our school and to bring me a new permit.

When the director of education came for a visit and saw with what enthusiasm our children were studying in a partially ruined building, he marvelled: "Sir, we cannot entice our Turkish boys to our palatial school buildings built with ample government funds. What a remarkable people you are that just returned from the wastelands, you can educate your children thus!" I thanked the official and accepted the permit, which I still keep today as a memento.

In a brief space of time a noticeable change took place among our students. Every morning I used to gather them into the church, give a few words of advice and encouragement, and teach them religious and patriotic songs. Our whole populace supported the project and was relieved and happy at the reclamation of these children, who once again were speaking their native Armenian with a respectable vocabulary, instead of Arabic, Kurdish, or Turkish vulgarities. Our children returned gradually from wild, primitive behavior to the ranks of civilized society.

I still remember a touching incident at the school, which reflects the sensitive spirit of the children. One day a boy named Aram started acting up during study time and was trying to make the children around him laugh. I called him to me and advised him to stop his antics and to study. A little later he did the same thing. This time I had him stand for half an hour. When he repeated a third time, I called him up and struck his hand with a stick saying, "Aram, my boy, I'm very sorry I have to punish you like this. Please be good now." When Aram went to his seat, a friend named Bedros who sat next to him said, "Aram, you know the Reverend loves us. When he hit you, did you say 'Thank you' to him? Quickly, go kiss his hand and say 'Thank you'!" Aram came up, kissed my hand, and thanked me. I then kissed his cheeks. Who would not kiss such a fine Armenian boy? Among the millions of schoolboys today, is it possible to find one single Aram or Bedros?

Morale was high. But alas! Again our success was shortlived. The cooperation of the officials proved transitory. The massacre of the French in Urfa turned out to be only one incident in what is now recognized as the Kemalist Revolution. Armenians had to face yet another set of persecutions. By the fall of 1920 we received word that the remnants of the Armenians of my hometown of Marash, including those who had returned there from exile with the hope of re-establishing their lives, had been subjected to another massacre after the French withdrawal there in the beginning of the year, just about the time the Turks were threatening the French in Urfa. Concerned about my brother Luther and sister Aghavni and their families, I wrote to the missionaries in Marash inquiring about my family. The answer arrived at the government office: "All Jernazians have been killed." I learned the details later. My brother Luther who had narrowly escaped death in the Massacre of 1895 and who had saved my life on that occasion, his wife Makruhi, and daughters Lydia and Marie were burned in their home. My sister Aghavni, her husband Nazaret, and two of their daughters — Dikranuhi and Azniv — were killed at the same time, but I never found out how they died. Their sons tried to escape. Krikor and Garabed succeeded. They tried to help Samuel who was hiding in the bushes, waiting for a safe time to run. His brothers signalled to him to lie low because of danger ahead, but he misunderstood, thinking they were signalling him to come out, and was shot. One daughter, Maria, had been married in September of 1919 and gone to Adana. She survived, and with her family and two brothers eventually moved to Buenos Aires. My niece Maria had made and given me a gift of a hand-embroidered white silk tie and a fine needlework watch fob when I left Marash for my pastorate at Urfa. This is another of the few precious mementos I have been able to save. My brother Dicran's widow Khatun had remarried after the illness and death of little Krikor in 1902. She and her husband Garabed Bilezikjian survived the massacre of 1920 and escaped first to Aleppo, then to Beirut. I met one son, also named Krikor, and his family in Boston during my pastorate there in the 1940s. Another son, Levon, settled in France. Khatun's younger sister Mary, husband Charles Koundakjian, and their sons were members of my Boston congregation.

Part IV
Prison and Release

31. Arrest and Imprisonment

B y 1921 I was the sole survivor of the Jernazian family. How long would I remain alive? Would Urfa share the final destiny of Marash? By the end of 1920 the political climate was once again becoming ominous. Although no gun collections or other acts of general discrimination were performed, government officials created opportunities to harass individuals.

Toward the end of January a messenger called to escort me to the *mutesarif*'s office. I went expecting the worst, but my apprehensions left me when His Honor simply asked me to let him have my Turkish-French dictionary. Of course, I obliged. But I thought perhaps the mutesarif was trying to do me a kindness and in this way was giving me a warning of things to come, so I took precautions. First, I buried my shotguns in a hole in our dirt roof. Then I disposed of certain papers that might be incriminating in case of a search. I gathered others, which I did not want destroyed, put them into a packet, and gave them to my mother-in-law. She placed them in our grain bin near the kitchen, for easy removal at a critical time.

My suspicions were confirmed two weeks later. On February 9, 1921, at 4:30 in the afternoon, after closing songs and prayers at school, I sent the students home as usual. Arriving home tired, I had just sat down to relax a little when suddenly there was a loud, staccato knock at the door. Without knowing who was there, I said to my wife, "When police come to arrest someone, this is how they knock," and I went downstairs. My mother-in-law was just opening the door, and I saw four policemen there who announced, "Effendi, you are to come with us." I could ask no questions. I knew my time had come. I simply agreed, "I will get my hat and come." Handcuffs placed on my wrists confirmed that this was an arrest.

At that moment my mother-in-law, realizing that an immediate search of our home was a possibility, quickly took out from the grain bin the papers we had hidden there, concealed them in her *shalvar* (baggy oriental slacks), and took them out the rear door. She managed to bury them in the rubble of the yard. Knowing that I was destined for death, I said my last farewell to my loved ones and went out.

They put me in solitary confinement. I spent that night praying and meditating without sleeping a moment. Early the next morning Marie took the risk of coming to visit me. She brought food and informed me that besides myself five others had been arrested: Karekin Effendi Turyekian, a pharmacist born in Harput and a resident of Urfa since childhood, a member of the Apostolic church; Arakel Turyekian, Karekin's sixteen-year-old younger brother; Vasil Sabagh, a merchant from Urfa, Catholic; Harutiun Dayarmanjian, a tailor from Urfa, Apostolic; and Hagop Devejian, a master-weaver from Urfa, Apostolic.

After keeping us in jail for one week in Urfa, one early morning they started us on the road to Diarbakir. Arakel, being very young, was released. Fortunately, our wives were permitted to hire donkeys for our journey. When Marie came to tell about arrangements for my donkey, she brought me a quilt, some food, and a Bible. I was permitted to keep this Bible since it was in Turkish (though with Armenian transliteration) and had been printed with permission from the Turkish government. Marie was able to tell me at this time the reason for our arrest. We ourselves were not told until months later at our trial. She had obtained the information from a Circassian *cadi* (Moslem ecclesiastical judge), a neighbor of Herr Eckart's, whose wife had become acquainted with Marie before our marriage and was fond of the "sweet little blue-eyed, blond Armenian girl." Shortly after my arrest Marie visited the cadi's wife and told her of the event, and asked if the cadi could give any enlightenment as to why I had been taken. The woman asked sympathetically, "Why do you think he was arrested? Can you think of anything that might have given them cause for suspicion?" Marie answered, "I can't think of anything except that we're Armenian." The lady acknowledged that as a reason but added that an incriminating picture had been found.

After the armistice, when several of us were preparing accommodations for the returning exiled Armenian women at the Monastery of St. Sarkis, we found unburied bones of Armenian martyrs all around the yard there. We gathered these bones and had a burial service. The Catholic priest at Urfa, Father Rafael, had taken a picture of the service. Turkish police had somehow gotten hold of a copy of that picture — perhaps while searching one of the homes — and used it as a pretext for our arrest. Marie protested, "Why, that's just a picture of a burial service," and explained the background. This explanation was obviously new to the woman. She went back to her husband to pass on the information. He appeared, and tried to console Marie: "*Allah kerim dir* [God is merciful] . . . Don't be afraid. Trust in Him." Most of those in the picture had, fortunately, departed from the city. Those of us who remained were arrested.

I had seen many dark and dismal days. Orphaned at an early age, I had experienced four massacres, always losing family members, and I was now the sole survivor of a family of four brothers and two sisters. Now this was the darkest and most discouraging of all. Not only I personally but the whole Jernazian family would be eliminated. The plight of my immediate family especially preyed upon my mind. What would happen to them? We were expecting our second child in six months. I might never see that child. Since 1915, no one who was arrested in Urfa and sent to Diarbakir returned alive. In fact, most were killed on the road soon after leaving Urfa. But Marie's expression at that last visit just before we were transported away from the prison in Urfa was reassuring. Her bravely cheerful countenance frequently came back to me during my imprisonment and reminded me that she had the strength to face all difficulties. My faith and hope in God were not extinguished in me, and these sustained me. With that same faith and hope Marie and her mother Hripsime also endured.

Our escorts to Diarbakir were a cavalry sergeant-major and three gendarmes on horseback. The sergeant was an acquaintance of mine and throughout the journey he was very good to us. When we passed through Sheytan Deresi, where thousands of Armenians before us including Zohrab and Vartkes had been slain, and nothing happened to us, our hope of remaining alive, at least for a time, was strengthened. When we stopped en route at Severeg, we were placed in a dark and dirty barn overnight. This was the first time since our arrest that my comrades and I were able to converse with each other and to encourage each other.

When we arrived at Diarbakir, we were taken to a military prison outside the city. A horses' stable in the fort had been converted into a prison — that is to say, the windows intended for horses had been boarded up. It was a dark barn filled to the door with prisoners. The air was putrid, the ground filthy, crawling with lice and vermin. There was no toilet, just a large jar. Twice a day permission was given for a very brief recess in the yard. If I were to be asked what is worse than what we imagine as Hell, I would have to say, "the military prison at Diarbakir." There was hardly room for 75 persons in that stable, but 150 people were crowded into it. With great difficulty we found just barely enough room to sit down. It was so dark in the prison that we could not tell whether it was day or night except by looking out of a tiny window in one corner of the room.

Most of the prisoners were either murderers or deserters from the army, while a few of us were political prisoners. Many had chains on their feet, and at every move they made, the clanging of the chains could be heard. On one side of me was a semi-nude Kurdish murderer. On the other side of me was the brother-in-law of Jahver Pasha, mentioned in the book and motion picture of Lawrence of Arabia. He had come from Syria to help the Turks in their battles against the French; but as soon as he had crossed the border, the Turkish military officials had robbed him and thrown him into jail at Diarbakir as a spy, refusing to let him write either to Jahver Pasha or to his wife. Also at the prison was an Indian notable called Sheikh Mohammed by the Turks. He, too, had been arrested as a spy.

We arrived at Diarbakir during the month of Ramadan, holy month of the Mohammedans; therefore, all court sessions were suspended. We had to wait until the end of Ramadan for our trial.

The prison was under the surveillance of a sergeant-major and twenty soldiers. The warden was an Arab major — a cruel, merciless one with a surly face. One day he came earlier than usual to inspect the prison. A prisoner named Ali Chavush (Sergeant) was standing in front of the small window, looking out. The major had seen him, entered with a thick stick in his hand, called Ali Chavush to come forward, and menaced, "You are planning to escape from jail. I am going to teach you a lesson now." He then began beating the prisoner and shouting, "They call me the Arab major. I make men cry out like a goat and writhe like a serpent." The poor young fellow Ali fainted and fell to the floor. No doubt our turn would come. I thought, "If the Turk Ali gets such a severe beating, how horrible will our share be? Most likely, we will be beaten to death." As a matter of fact, my friends and I were not beaten. Ali Chavush, together with a companion, did eventually escape. I will tell about that later.

32. Preliminary Trial

E ven if we were not hanged immediately or beaten to death, we could not hope to remain alive long under the existing conditions in that prison at Diarbakir. Within one week I became ill and thought this might be the end for me, but fortunately my condition proved not to be serious, and I recovered in a few days. One morning the sergeant-major came into our barn to take a few prisoners out to the yard for a work detail. Some bribed him to avoid being taken out; I asked to be taken out. The man was amazed. But this was a real opportunity for me. When I went out, my God! What clean, fresh air there was! I worked in the yard until evening, enjoying every minute. The soldier guarding me advised, "Sir, sit down occasionally, but when you see the sergeant, work fast." When I returned into the prison that evening, I felt that the color had returned to my cheeks.

We needed most of all to communicate with our families, but how? By a miracle of God a way appeared. Diarbakir was a military center, and a headquarters was located there. One day one of the headquarters staff, a lieutenant named Kiazim Effendi, came unexpectedly to the prison to see me and offered to help me: "Reverend Sir, two years ago you did me a great favor which I can never forget. Now it is my turn to help you. Tell me what I can do for you." I knew him in Urfa as a civilian when he was the vali's chauffeur, but I could not remember what favor I had done. I was glad to see him, thanked him very much, and asked if it might be possible to take a letter to my wife in Urfa and to bring hers to me. He was more than willing: "Gladly! Write your letter in Armenian. Don't be afraid. Your letter will get into no one's hand but your wife's. I will bring her answer to you. I will return in two days to get your letter. I will find a reason to use the commander's car to go to Urfa and back."

Two days later Kiazim Effendi came. I put my letter and those of my colleagues into one envelope and handed the packet to him. A week later he returned with replies from our wives and told me about his visit to our home. He had told my two-year-old daughter Alice, "Alice, my little girl, I am going to bring you another letter from your father." Little Alice had answered, "No, I don't want any letters from you. I want my daddy. Bring my daddy to me." The young Turkish soldier's eyes filled up. Throughout my twenty-one months of imprisonment Kiazim Effendi carried our letters back and forth several times. Thanks to him and to two other sources of help, we survived. Marie earned money by sewing. She was able to send us some food, clothing, and other items as well as money through missionaries. Also, one of my companions, Vasil, arranged to buy food through a Kurdish chief who had connections on the outside.

We learned from our families that all were alive and well. The Turkish government had not given them any trouble. Only the police had come several times to our home, searched it, and gathered most of my books and writings and taken them away. Officer Ghadri Effendi, who knew me well, had said to Marie, "Why does your husband have so many books? Isn't one Bible enough? Our *hojas* [teachers] have just the Koran." What could she answer?

One day when the month of Ramadan was over, we were taken in chains before the military court. First, our indictment was read: "Disturbed the peace internally and externally. Disgraced the Ottoman nation and sultanate before the world." As proof of this accusation the court produced the photograph taken at the St. Sarkis Monastery at Urfa at the time of the burial of the scattered bones and skulls of the martyred Armenians. There were two captions on the picture. One was in Armenian at the top right, a statement of Krikor Zohrab: "We are passing on, but the nation has 400,000 orphans. Save them." The other was in the center of the picture, in English: "The Bases of Civilization in the Near East. Armenian skulls. Urfa, 1914-1919."

Fortunately, we had heard from Marie before leaving Urfa that the police chief had found that picture, in which we all appeared, and accused us through it. Again, luckily, we were placed together in the prison at Diarbakir, so that we were able to plan our defense together. Since I had conducted the burial as a clergyman, I would receive the bulk of the pressure. We had to deny our guilt in a convincing and logical manner.

First, each of my colleagues was briefly questioned. Since they did not know Turkish very well, I had written out proper Turkish statements using Armenian letters, and my friends learned them and used them as needed.

When my turn arrived, the chief judge of the court asked my name and profession, then showed me the picture of the skulls. "What is this picture?" Calmly and in good Turkish I answered, "Your Honor, we did not kill them." The man was taken by surprise, and with a stern look said, "I know that you did not kill them, but why did you have this picture taken?" I said, "Your Honor, that is a photo of the burial ceremony of the unburied bones of Armenians killed at the St. Sarkis Monastery during the battles at Urfa. Sir, you know that although music and pictures are not allowed in the worship services according to the rules of Islam, these are permitted according to Christian rules and are a part of the services. Since the beginning, our benevolent Ottoman government has allowed us to conduct our services according to our rules and customs. Thus, we often have photos taken during weddings and funerals for remembrance."

The judge continued, "Sir, tell the truth. What would one say if he were to look at this picture?" I answered, "He would say that they all died at the same time." The judge felt insulted and, throwing a sharp glance at me, continued, "You had this picture taken in order to show the Europeans and Americans that the Turk has thus mercilessly killed you in masses." I answered, "Your Honor, this picture was taken several months after the Europeans and Americans came to Urfa. On their way from Palestine and Syria to Urfa they saw thousands more of these bones. What purpose, then, would a picture with a few bones serve?"

The judge, in a tone partly embarrassed and partly disdainful, said, "You did a pretty good job of convincing us, but what about these captions? What is their significance?" I answered, "Your Honor, I do not remember who wrote those captions, but the meaning of each is clear. The caption at the top is in Armenian. It is a quotation from our representative in the Ottoman legislature, a man respected by everyone, Krikor Zohrab. Translated, it says, 'We are passing on, but our nation has 400,000 orphans. Save them.' The same admonition to care for orphans is given to us both in the Holy Koran and the Holy Bible. It is purely a godly and humanitarian proverb which the honorable Zohrab repeated. As for the caption in the middle in English, it is translated 'These are the skulls of Armenians who are the basis of culture in the Near East.' This signifies that in this land our Turkish compatriots have special ability and influence in political and military matters, whereas we Armenians have special talents in the crafts and businesses by which we serve this country, which is part of the Near East. There is absolutely no political significance in either of those two captions. Also, on Moslem graves a verse from the holy scripture is inscribed. On Christian graves the epitaph refers to some good work or outstanding quality of the deceased. I am sure, Your Honor, that you are familiar with these facts, too."

Members of the court reacted with heightened interest and curiosity at such unexpected answers from a young Protestant minister. The judge then mockingly continued, "Very well, Sir, you got out of that one, too. Now tell me why you did not attend our government schools and chose to get your education at American schools." I answered, "Your Honor, you have permitted Americans to open schools in this country and have given us freedom to attend them. In Istanbul and Beirut Mohammedan students also attend schools administered by Americans and other foreigners. Furthermore, my diploma from the American College at Tarsus has been certified by the governor of Adana, and under his order has been signed by the state secretary of education. And I had one other reason. I wanted to become a Christian preacher. I could not become a Christian preacher by attending a Moslem school. For these reasons I received my education in American schools." The judge, perplexed, then suggested, "Then are we the guilty ones for punishing innocent ones like you?" I protested, "God forbid, Your Honor. We do witness before God and you that, born and raised in this country, we are obedient citizens who request that you permit us freedom to bring our humble share of services to our country."

Repeatedly surprised and bewildered by my answers, the judge was constantly trying to trap me by his questioning. But I was always mindful of Christ's promise in Matthew 10:19: "But when they deliver you up, take no thought how or what ye shall speak: for it shall be given you in that same hour what ye shall speak." I do testify that this word of Christ was fulfilled for me as for many believers who shared my fortune. The judge made one last effort to trip me up: "Sir, if you really are a loyal subject, tell us who the leaders of the Hunchak and Dashnak committees in Urfa were." I said, "Your Honor, I am the preacher of the Armenian Protestant congregation in Urfa. Ask me the names of those I have baptized, married, or buried, and I can tell you. As for the names of the Hunchak and Dashnak political leaders, please consult the police chief of Urfa. That information comes under his duties." To my great relief, the judge made no further effort to extract the names from me, and asked no further questions. Another inexplicable phenomenon!

Thoroughly disgruntled, the judge concluded, "Go back to prison, and you will be called again sixty days later." The guards handcuffed us again and took us back to the military prison to wait another sixty days. Incidentally, the handcuffs varied in size. I always extended my hands toward the large ones because on the way I could slip my hands out and walk comfortably, then slip them back in toward the end of the road.

When we were back in prison, my friend Hagop Devejian inquired, "Badveli, how could you give such clever answers so fearlessly? Weren't you afraid they might send us to the gallows immediately?" I told him, "Hagop, if they have decided to hang us, as I'm sure they have, they'll hang us anyway. Our cowering before them or giving them wretched answers will not cause them to change their minds in the slightest. Let them say, at least, 'We hanged five fearless *giavoors*'. That will bring honor to our holy faith and to our nation. May God give us strength to be brave martyrs, if we must be martyrs."

33. Stones from the Fortress

S ince Diarbakir had become one of the country's large military centers, the need for a new government building was felt. The men who worked the local quarries to produce the building materials had all been Armenians, and they had all been killed. Turkish officials devised another way to obtain building stones — to tear down the fortress of the city and to build the new building from the stones obtained there. A few Armenian carpenters and masons had been allowed to live; they would be available to put up the building.

So that the officials themselves might pocket the money earmarked for tearing down the fortress, they conceived the idea of using prisoners as slave labor. Early one morning the Arab major, a sergeant-major, and twenty-five soldiers took one hundred of us from the prison to the fortress. They lined us up before the wall. The Arab major looked us over sternly and warned, "You are surrounded with soldiers. Don't ever think of escaping. You will be shot on the spot." He gave the sergeant some instructions and left. While we were still in line, the sergeant picked up a small rock from the ground and turning to us, said, "Look at me. This rock is my conscience." Throwing the rock away, he added, "I have just thrown away my conscience. Now I am going to curse at you and whip you; don't be surprised. I threw away my conscience." And he really did shout, curse, and whip until evening.

A cartload of tools was brought for us to use in tearing down the wall. The soldiers surrounding us watched us closely to shoot any who might try to escape. The prisoners were marched upon the wall to remove the stones. The work had just begun when the sergeant came to me and gave me special instructions: "You don't look like one who should tear walls down. Take this pitcher and bring water to this bunch from that spring nearby."

Before long, two of the prisoners succeeded in tricking one of the guards by saying, "A woman is waiting for us inside this wall; let us go see her and come back." The naive soldier believed them and obligingly let them go. They went in and never came out. The guard became impatient after a while, and he went after them; but all he could find inside were the chains from their feet. The prisoners had disappeared. These two were the Turk Ali Chavush, who had been beaten earlier for looking out the window, and his Armenian companion Avedis Chavush. Both *chavushes* had deserted from the Mosul-Bagdad front, robbing and killing Turkish officers on the way. They had finally been arrested and sentenced to death, and were awaiting final disposition of their sentence. The poor soldier came back dejected. He knew what his fate would be.

Towards evening the Arab major came back, saw that the prisoners were sweating hard at their task but that only forty or fifty stones had been removed. Shaking his head, he came and stood near me and ordered all the prisoners to come down and line up. When we were all looking at him with great curiosity, he said, "Look, boys, a nation that lived two thousand years ago built this wall. We of the twentieth century can't even tear down the wall they built. You can see how backward we are." With those closing words we prisoners, flanked by columns of soldiers, began our march back toward the accursed dungeon. When the roll was called, Ali and Avedis Chavush were absent. Their guard was brought before the major. The poor soldier was mercilessly beaten and thrown into prison in chains. We learned afterwards from the major's clerk that a month later a letter had come to the major from the two chavushes. They had written, "Honorable Major, we have arrived safe and sound at Aleppo. Give our regards to our imprisoned friends. May they have the same luck we had."

Not long after this, one day early in the morning, there was a great commotion in front of the prison. The Arab major and a group of military officers opened the door and began counting the prisoners. When they found none missing, they went back out. We heard afterwards that the sergeant-major who was guarding the prison had deserted at night, together with the twenty soldiers assisting him, and gone to Mosul. The prisoners bewailed the loss of this opportunity to escape themselves.

34. From Prison to Prison

The sixty days we were told to wait passed by, but we were not summoned as expected. After being in the military prison for five months, we were transferred to the large jail near the government buildings in the city, and our case was assigned to the criminal court. This jail had several advantages. There were six large, barn-like rooms with dirt floors as in the other prison, but these were arranged around a large, open court with a fountain in the center. Each room had one or two windows with iron grills facing the courtyard. Each room had actual toilet facilities of its own, poor as they might be. During the day we were allowed to spend a number of hours in the yard. These improvements helped considerably for us to remain alive during the sixteen more months that we were there.

The warden was from Bitlis, a Turk who hated Armenians. Taking us to the worst of the rooms (or, more accurately, stables), he showed us the area near the latrine and said, "This is your place." Suddenly one of the prisoners from the other side of the room bellowed, "Warden, where is your room?" The warden answered, "Upstairs." The prisoner, a large Kurd named Kelegji Muhammed Agha, shouted, "Then get lost and go to your room. You have the right only to say that these men must stay in this room. It's none of your business what part of the room they stay in." The warden was frightened and left. Muhammed Agha ordered the Kurds near him, "Move over, all of you, and make room for these gentlemen!" And he took me next to him.

We were happy to be relieved of the odors of the latrine and to be near the window, but we weren't quite sure whether Muhammed Agha did us this kindness because he cared for us or to do us some harm. We wanted to be optimistic and gave him our thanks. He turned to me reassuringly: "Hoja Effendi, don't worry; as long as I am in this jail, nobody is going to hurt any of you." I thanked him again, for in this jail amidst thieves and murderers a protective ally would be welcome. Many Armenians had been killed there. Soon afterwards when Kelegji Muhammed Agha told us his story, we were completely sure of his sincerity.

Who was he? He was a Kurdish resident of Diarbakir, who knew Turkish well. He transported goods down the Tigris River between Diarbakir and Mosul with a leather-hulled ferryboat. One evening he said his customary good-bye to his wife, kissed his two-year-old son, and left. When he arrived at his boat, he found that part of the cargo to be transported had not yet arrived. So he returned home to start out the next day with a full load. He arrived home near midnight and was surprised to find a light on. Just a few hours ago his wife and son were fine. What could be wrong? He began to have some suspicions. Taking off his shoes, he quietly went up the outside stairs and, looking in the window, saw one of his neighbors with his wife. He entered immediately and snapped at the man, "Don't say a word!" Then turning to his wife he said, "Woman, I am your lawfully wedded husband. I love you. I have always been faithful to you and cared for you, and I am younger and more handsome than this worthless man. What a despicable thing it is you are doing when I have hardly put my foot out the door! You have no right to live." And he thrust the knife into his wife's bosom. Then turning to the man, "Shameless wretch, why don't you go to someone filthy like yourself instead of coming near someone innocent like my wife? You have absolutely no right to live! If I let you live, who knows how many more innocent persons you will defile?" He killed the neighbor, too. He took the little boy over to his sister's and early in the morning went before the judge and said, "Your Honor, I am going to tell you personally what happened to me and what I did. If you are an honorable man, commend me and let me go take care of my only child. If you, too, have no sense of honor, then put me in jail." Muhammed Agha added, "Hoja Effendi, this judge was shameless, too. He sentenced me to fifteen years in jail."

That night we were able to sleep more comfortably than at any time the last five months, because we had room enough to lie down. Early in the morning the doors of the room were opened, and all the Mohammedans went out around the fountain in the center of the courtyard to perform their ablutions. They washed, came back in, and stood in line for prayers. I knelt down, and began reading my Bible and praying. I was still allowed to keep my Bible. My companion Hagop Devejian was concerned: "Badveli, my dear fellow, is this the time to read and pray? I am afraid these savages will come back after their ritual and beat you up." I said, "Hagop, even if they beat me or kill me, I am going to read my Bible and say my prayers." When the ritual was over, a wealthy young Kurd called Hakim Agha came to us and asked Hagop, "Comrade, what's your name?" "My name is Hagop," answered Mr. Devejian. Hakim Agha continued, "Look here, Hagop, if you are a Christian, why didn't you pray with the *hoja*? If you are Moslem, why didn't you come with us for the *namaz* [Moslem ritual prayer]? We don't want atheists here."

I had to think of a way to defend Mr. Devejian, so I explained, "Hakim Agha, we read the Bible first and then pray. Since we have only one Bible, I read and prayed first. Now Hagop and my other friends will read and pray." The Kurd said, "Pardon me, Hoja Effendi, I did not know your rules."

Hakim Agha and another wealthy Kurd, Mustafa Agha, were leaders of a group that had rioted in the city. Thirty of their men had been imprisoned with them. They had attacked a prison in Diarbakir, killed two gendarmes, and taken all the Kurdish prisoners there out with them. The Turkish government had pursued them with a battalion of soldiers and arrested them. A year later they were all freed for a bribe of three hundred gold pieces (fifteen hundred dollars). They counted the money in my presence. I was later informed that the Turkish Criminal Court had given their release on the following basis: "Since the attack was made by the whole Jemi Ghafor group, it was not clear as to whose bullet killed those two gendarmes; therefore the imprisoned thirty individuals cannot be personally liable."

After the prayers, we began to get acquainted with others of the more than one thousand prisoners in this prison. The Kurds came over to us and one asked me, "Hoja Effendi, *messeleteh chiyeh* [what is your problem]?" I said, "Khalo [Uncle — a customary salutation in Kurdish], we have disgraced the Turkish government before the world and have disturbed the peace internally and externally." They all laughed. One of them spoke up: "Ha! The Turks have disgraced themselves. There is no need for others to disgrace them." In one or two hours all the prisoners in our room knew who we were and that we would be hanged soon.

It was our turn to find out who the others were, so I began asking them one by one, "Khalo, messeleteh chiyeh?" The majority of prisoners were Kurds. There were a substantial number of Turks. All were thieves, robbers, murderers, and political prisoners from Konia. Almost all were sentenced to fifteen years or more. There were also two Greeks. Mr. Alkibiades had been an interpreter aboard a French warship. In response to a Turkish demand from Constantinople, the French had surrendered him to the Turkish government who had sentenced him to life imprisonment. The other Greek was a fearless engineer named Bedo from Konia. He was accused of throwing two Turkish military officials into the furnace of a train. Although there had been no eye-witnesses, he was sentenced to life imprisonment.

The most distinguished prisoner in the complex was the Kurd Abdullah Agha, thirty-five years old, wealthy, handsome, and well-mannered but extremely cruel. He had killed thirty-six men, for what reason we did not know, and had finally been arrested.

There were four Kurds near me in the room. They had killed and robbed a Turkish captain and five soldiers. One of them said to me, "Hoja Effendi, I know it is a sin to kill good men like you, but is it a sin to kill those cruel Turks?" In those days the Turkish government had begun to persecute the Kurds, too.

I asked another young man, "Khalo, messeleteh chiyeh?" He said, "I killed two men, and they've had me in jail for five years. That's not fair."

There was also a Turkish hoja in our room. One day I noticed that he was picking the lice off his person and placing them in an envelope. Surprised, I asked why he did not kill the harmful bugs instead of collecting them. He said, "Well, my son, after all, lice are living creatures; it's a sin to kill them." I asked, "Hoja, why are you in prison?" The hoja answered, "I had an argument with my wife. She got me very angry, so I killed her." Again surprised, I asked, "Hoja, was not your wife as worthy as a bug? How is it that you spare the bug that bites you but kill the wife who serves you?" He said, "Effendi, let's not get too deep."

In another room in the prison was Bekir Effendi, a well-to-do Turk from Diarbakir. This man had once invited to his home two wealthy men who had come to Diarbakir for business, had fed and entertained them, then killed and robbed them. He had had their bodies thrown into a well on the abandoned property of an Armenian. He had two wives. One day he had a fight with one of his wives, who became very angry and went directly to the chief of police to expose her husband. The police found the corpses in the well. That same day they arrested Bekir Effendi and brought him to jail. I said to him, "Bekir Effendi, your case is very serious; I'm afraid your punishment will be very heavy." The man laughed and said, "Hoja Effendi, Allah is merciful." Six months later he came to me and announced, "Hoja Effendi, tomorrow I am going home. May you have similar luck." Through his brother he had arranged bribes: 50 gold pieces for the judge, 25 gold pieces for each of two other court personnel, and 10 gold pieces for each of two policemen. Charges were dropped against him, and he was released as innocent. On what grounds? At night the police had replaced the two corpses of the men with the bodies of two dogs they had killed. The court ordered a second investigation, and the inspecting officials had made a report stating, "Although two corpses were discovered in the designated well, it was found that these were not the bodies of men but of dogs. Therefore, Bekir Effendi is entirely innocent."

Every one of those hundreds of prisoners had his own special story, extremely interesting. There are different worlds on this earth. One cannot understand a world until he lives in it. Prison is an unnatural world, and very few really know what life is like in prisons —especially Turkish prisons.

35. Survival in Prison

The Criminal Court, it seemed, wanted to keep our group of five in jail for an extended period of time before hanging us. Every one or two months we Armenians were taken to the court, pressured to confess, then returned to jail without a sentence when we did not confess. So we had to be patient and try to stay alive, hoping for a miracle. Although we were threatened many times, we were fortunate that we were not beaten and were, at times, even treated politely. The authorities felt, no doubt, that in this manner we could be persuaded to confess, or to give incriminating information about others.

Survival in prison was difficult because of the filth, the polluted air, the poor and meagre food, the mental strain of boredom and of concern for our families, and the violent nature of many inmates. Most of the prisoners made no effort to be clean, and vermin swarmed about them. Those of us who tried to keep clean were constantly fighting these insects as well as the filth that produced them. The air in the room was polluted and in the summer months unbearably hot. The cigarette smoke and odor bothered me very much. My friends suggested that if I would take up smoking myself, it wouldn't irritate me that much. But I didn't want to smoke, so that I could more effectively advise and warn the opium smokers. I was pleased that I was able to help some.

As for food, each day we were given only one piece of dry bread which often resembled cow's dung and tasted bitter. Often weak prisoners would die while waiting for their trial. The prisoners next to them would not report the death until the stench of the corpse became intolerable, so that they might receive the bread rations of the dead, either to eat or to sell for money to buy tobacco. We were fortunate that we were able once or twice a week to have food brought in from the outside — sometimes through our friend Kelegji Muhammed Agha and sometimes through a Mohammedan priest who used to come to lead the prisoners in their prayer ritual. Of course, we paid them; and I always wrote up the accounts for Muhammed Agha, since he did not know how to read and write. One day the brother of one of the Kurdish prisoners brought him a lamb. The lamb was butchered outside and the meat brought in to sell. A number of the Turks and Kurds in the prison came to buy the meat. Each one bought half a pound or more, but none paid in cash; they all promised to pay later. I went over, too, and putting ten *kurush* into the hand of the Kurd who was selling the meat, I said, "Khalo, please give me a pound of meat." The Kurd took the money, looked at me with a smile, and turning to the prisoners, said, "Look here, everybody, this Armenian Hoja Effendi is the only one up till now who put the money into my hands for the meat — not anybody else. As Allah is my witness, when the Armenian is gone, blessing is gone."

Inactivity is another of the curses of Turkish prisons. At this jail we had no opportunity to volunteer for work detail. Day and night we had to sit and sit, then alternately lie down. Our only movement came during the short space of time we were allowed out in the courtyard. I would continually pace back and forth in my little corner of the yard. Gradually I found ways to occupy my time indoors. Through a Turkish military officer at the prison, Nzamedin Effendi, I was able to get hold of a French grammar book. I spent about an hour a day studying French. I wrote letters for some poor Kurds; often I supplied the paper and stamps. Because of this I acquired, in addition to Kelegji Muhammed Agha, many friends among the prisoners who always looked after my welfare. I taught one of my Armenian friends, Vasil, how to read and write Turkish; and my friends and I discussed patriotic, religious, and historical subjects. Often when I would be reading my Bible, prisoners near me, especially the Kurds, wanted to hear what I was reading. Once when I was reading from Christ's sermon on the mount, one of the Kurds asked, "Hoja Effendi, you people have such a wonderful book. Why do we kill you?" I said, "Khalo, our book is very good; so are we. You are bad for killing us." They all shook their heads: "You're very right, Hoja. We are bad for having massacred you and ruined the country." Though these men were coarse, illiterate, and easily provoked to criminal action, they had a certain childlike simplicity about them and frequently revealed an appreciation for morality and for education. Since in their eyes I was a symbol of both, they treated me with respect. One or two hours a day I visited with the Kurdish *aghas*, and from time to time I visited with others who invited me.

A man from Diarbakir by the name of Sukdi Effendi, the secretary of the mayor of the city of Baker-Maden, had been jailed for bribery. (I don't know the circumstances which would have singled him out for prosecution when bribery was a commonly accepted practice among officials.) Sukdi Effendi had presented a mathematical problem to the prisoners in his room for anyone to solve. He had told them that it was so difficult that none of the officials in Baker-Maden had been able to solve it. No one in his room had been able to solve it. One of them suggested asking the hoja from Urfa. So they presented it to me. Using simple algebraic principles, I promptly solved it. They were all amazed, and from that day on, their respect and sympathy toward me increased.

On a number of occasions we witnessed the violence of the prisoners. Some of these incidents I still remember well. One day just before noon the doors of the prison rooms were open, and most of the prisoners were seated in the courtyard. Some were chatting together; some were playing cards or backgammon. Two Kurds got into an argument and soon began striking each other. One of them was of the Berveri tribe, the other, Beshari. Suddenly the hundreds of quietly seated Berveri and Beshari Kurds in the prison arose and began beating each other. The agha of the Berveri Kurds on one side would say, *"Lo, lekhi* [Hit'em, boys]." The agha of the Beshari Kurds on the other side would also say, "Lo, lekhi." And thus a horrible fight began. They threw water jugs at each other's heads, and the bursting of the jugs sounded like the burst of cannon. The quiet prison became a battlefield. The agha of the Berveris said to me, "Hoja Effendi, you and your friends stay near me and don't be afraid. No one will hit you." And, in truth, no one touched us.

Presently about a dozen policemen entered and tried to stop the fight, whereupon the Kurds stopped beating each other and together attacked the police. In a few minutes all the police were flat on the ground. Then, again, while the two chiefs were once again saying "Lo, lekhi," the Kurds were hitting each other even more savagely. Many were injured or fell exhausted to the ground. The warden promptly requested help from the governor and from the military commander. Quickly two hundred soldiers came and surrounded the prison. The warden called out to the prisoners, "Kurds, if you do not stop fighting immediately, I am going to shoot all of you down." I said to the Kurdish agha beside me, "Agha, the Turk has no mercy. It will be too bad for you. Why don't you stop the fighting?" The agha agreed: "You're right, Hoja Effendi, the Turk has no mercy." Calling the opposing agha to him, he explained his viewpoint. The two aghas stood side by side, raised their right hands, and said, *"Lo, hes eh* [That's enough, boys]." The fighting stopped at once. Police and orderlies came and removed the wounded from the ground and tended their wounds. All the fighters resumed their peaceful positions and began carrying on again like brothers, continuing their games and conversations as though they were not the ones who had been fighting. I was amazed and told the agha who defended us, "Khalo, I don't understand what just happened. Why did all of you fight, and how did all of you suddenly become reconciled so that you are speaking together again and playing like brothers?" The agha explained. "Hoja Effendi, this is the rule of our Kurds: anytime that we see one of our tribe fighting with someone from another tribe, without questioning whose fault it is, we must immediately fight against anyone from the other tribe that might be near us. If we stay out of it, we are considered cowardly and deserters, and if at any future time we might be in trouble, no one will come to help us."

Another time, in one of the rooms of the prison some stealing was going on. Each day someone's shoes, someone's hat, someone else's jacket would disappear. This would be reported to the warden, but nothing was done about it. The Kurds in that room suspected a Turk named Ali. He was in prison for theft, anyway. The Kurds took turns keeping secret vigil at night. One night a watchman saw Ali raise his head and look around. He then saw

Ali slowly crawl over to a Turk, take his shoes, and hide them under his own jacket. In the morning when everyone went to the courtyard to wash up, Ali wrapped the stolen shoes in his shirt and went to hand them to his wife who was waiting just outside the front door. Just then the Kurd who had been watching him grabbed the packet from him and seizing Ali by the collar dragged him inside. Ali's wife ran away. Soon afterwards we noticed that there was much confusion in the room. The Kurds closed the door, and everyone soon learned what happened inside. They made Ali stand in the middle of the room. The leader of the room asked those who had lost items one by one, "What did you lose?" Accordingly he stripped Ali of each item as mentioned and gave it to the person robbed of it, until the thief Ali was totally naked. The prisoners in the room then filed past Ali and spat in his face. The warden tried to rescue Ali, but he was threatened with being seized if he tried to intervene, so he was too frightened to do anything further.

One of the policemen went to Ali's home and found the lost items. The wife had bundled them up and was just about to leave to sell them in the market. The police brought the bundle to the prison, returned the items to the rightful owners, and Ali was then allowed to remain unmolested. Needless to say, he gave no further trouble. Such swift and proper justice I have never seen anywhere.

36. A Jailbreak That Failed

One day the Kurds in our room approached the Greek engineer: "Bedo, you have to help us break out of the prison and escape." Bedo answered, "First of all, I don't trust you Kurds to keep a secret. Secondly, I am Greek; if we get caught, they'll surely hang me." The Kurds threatened to strangle him if he refused. He said to me, "Badveli, I can never cope with these Kurds. Risking all dangers, I shall have to help them."

This plan of the prisoners put the lives of us five Armenians in jeopardy also. We could not escape, since our families were in Urfa. They would be threatened. But even if we did not try to escape, the Turkish government would hold us accountable for not having told them about the plot. So, keeping his promise to offer us protection whenever necessary, Kelegji Muhammed Agha somehow promptly managed to have us transferred to another room. I learned later how the escape operation was conducted.

Three things were necessary for the jailbreak: short iron rods with sharp points to dig with, pieces of wood to cover the hole, and daggers and pistols to use if necessary at the time of the escape. Muhammed Agha and several other influential Kurds succeeded within two weeks in having their wives and sisters bring two iron rods, eight daggers, and five pistols. The women hid these in their bundles of clothes. When they brought the bundles, the Kurds would not allow them to be examined. They told the guard at the door, "Don't touch my wife's hand." The guard, afraid of what a jealous husband might do, let her pass without inspecting the bundle. Also, some prisoners had pieces of wood brought in under the pretext of needing them to burn for heating water for washing clothes. Actually, of course, this wood was to cover the opening of the hole during the day. As soon as all the items were ready, the project was begun. First, all the prisoners in the room knelt down and, placing hands on the Koran, vowed to work together and to keep the secret. Under Bedo's direction they began to dig near a post in the center of the room. This was done after sunset, and in order to distract the guards, a group of Kurds kept singing and dancing. The dirt that was dug out at night was spread over the floor of the room. During the day the hole was covered over with boards, and a sickly old man was made to lie down on it.

The digging went on for days and weeks, but the guards did not notice that the floor was rising gradually. A tunnel large enough to hold twenty to twenty-five men at a time was dug. Bedo examined it and found it adequate. The outer end of the tunnel had reached the wall of an outside pit, just as planned. The prisoners were delighted that they would escape from prison and breathe freely once more in their mountains. They wanted to get out that very night. Bedo advised, "Tonight is not a good time to escape. The air is too clear. The guards will easily see you and kill you. Wait for a cloudy night." It was of no use. The majority voted to get out that night. They warned, "If you don't let us leave tonight, we will tell the warden about the whole thing." This ridiculous threat overcame the good sense of the minority, and the opposition had to give in. They drew lots to determine the order of filing out. Again they swore by the Koran that those getting out first would wait for the rest so that all could run away together.

They descended into the tunnel one by one. The first one to put his head out saw that a soldier was standing right near the pit and looking toward the hole. The prisoner immediately withdrew, and all of them returned into the room cursing their luck and piling up rocks and dirt behind the exit. When the guards heard the commotion, they came to find out what the noise was all about. The prisoners boasted, "Don't you know? We dug out of the jail." Bedo's misgivings were confirmed; these impulsive Kurds could never keep a secret. The police thought the prisoners were joking but, upon investigation, found the hole and reported it to the warden.

Ironically, as it turned out, the guard outside had not seen the hole. He was down on the ground looking for a lost bullet. Soldiers immediately arrived from the armory and surrounded the prison. In the morning came the governor, the chief judge of the Criminal Court, the military commander, and other officials. When they entered and examined the hole and tunnel, they said, "Digging this hole is not the work of you Kurds. Tell the truth; who was your engineer? They answered, "Bedo, the Greek."

All the prisoners in that room were taken out into the courtyard one at a time and whipped. We could see them from our room. When it was Bedo's turn, they made him lie down. Then two policemen, each with a large stick in his hand, began to beat him. They beat him so much that they thought he must be either dead or unconscious, since he was not making a sound. They finally stopped. Bedo suddenly sat up and asked, "Gentlemen, did you get tired? May I get up now?" Everyone was amazed, and when the policemen resumed the beating, all the prisoners shouted, "Commander Bey, have you no decency? That's enough. Shame on you for wanting to beat such a brave man more!" The warden interrupted, "If it hadn't been for this Bedo, you would not have been able to break out like this." Bedo taunted, "Warden, my job is to escape, and your job is to stop me. What kind of chief are you that we were able to dig such a large hole without your even noticing it?" The commander turned to the warden and scolded, "Hold your tongue, you miserable wretch! They've dug a hole in the room right under your very nose, and you haven't even seen it. You don't deserve your position at all."

A month later amnesty was granted to all political prisoners from Konia. Among them was Bedo. Bedo's fame had spread throughout the city and the surrounding towns. When he was about to leave the prison, a Kurdish *agha* came galloping into town and accosted him: "I want you, Bedo, for a time at least, to be my guest and bodyguard so that my enemies may respect me." Bedo accepted the offer, mounted the horse which the agha had brought for him, and rode off with the Kurd.

37. A Spark of Hope

W e were expecting the birth of our second child six months after my arrest. As the weeks passed in prison, and as hope for my survival diminished, I prayed every day, "My God, if it is Thy will, please grant us a son so that the Jernazian name may not be lost." The news for which I was waiting finally came toward the end of August of 1921. Marie wrote, "The Lord gave us a beautiful, healthy son. What shall we name him?" I immediately thought of Anna, the mother of the prophet Samuel. When God granted her wish and gave her a son, she called him Samuel, which in Hebrew means "God heard my voice." I wrote a letter to my newborn son:

> My Darling Samuel,
> Welcome. In the dark prison cell you spread a ray of happiness over my heart. It is very likely that I may never be able to see you in this world, but I am sure that God will be your Father and under the loving care of your mother and grandmother, you will be a good child, bringing honor to your family and to your nation. I do have a spark of hope in my heart that I may one day actually hug you and love you. Welcome, our one and only Samuel!
> Your father who yearns for you.

Throughout the remaining months in jail, I was buoyed up by this news, prayerful that I might some day be reunited with my family. Under predictable circumstances, I had no hope of remaining alive. My companions and I just wondered whether we would be hanged or shot. Our bodies weakened together with our hopes. My hair literally turned white. Forgetting about ourselves, we worried about our families, wondering what would become of them.

One day a rumor went through the prison that the chief judge of the Criminal Court had been replaced by Ismael Bey, the Cypriot from Urfa, in whose court I had served as interpreter, and who had been sympathetic toward me. When Ismael Bey saw the name Ephraim Jernazian on the list of prisoners, he directed his deputy to bring me to him. The warden allowed me to go with the guard.

When Ismael Bey saw us enter the room, he told the guard, "You wait outside." He also dismissed the other officials around him. He expressed regret over my plight: "Vaiz Effendi, I am very sorry that you have been subjected to this misfortune. I am going to free you from prison. At the public trial I am going to have to deal with you sternly so that the other members of the court will not be suspicious, but don't be concerned about that." I said, "Your Honor, I am very grateful. May God give you recompense. I have four friends with me; I hope we will all be freed together." Ismael Bey assured me, "Of course. I am going to give the verdict in such a manner that you will all go back to Urfa under guard and will be interned there until the final decree comes from Mustafa Kemal Pasha's headquarters. I know that the decree will be death by hanging. Therefore, you must immediately cross the border in any way you can. Go to America if you can; if not, go to Beirut. God be with you."

Again I expressed my deep appreciation to Ismael Bey before returning to prison with my police escort. I was impatient to reveal this good news to my friends who were anxiously waiting. When I told them the story, we praised God in unison, as the hope for freedom was reborn in us.

Since our families were in Urfa, it would be difficult to escape after going to Urfa. I therefore wrote Marie, "November 27 is the final day of our trial. Go directly to Aleppo since my uncle is there." She answered, "How do you expect us to go farther away from you? It will be impossible to communicate with you."

I wrote a second time, saying, "For my sake, you must do as I say." Fortunately, in those days Kemal Pasha permitted Armenians to go out of Turkey. It suited his purposes to get as many more Armenians out of the country as possible. Taking advantage of that permission, many Armenians were finding ways to depart, since it was becoming increasingly obvious that it would no longer be possible to remain in Turkey and live as an Armenian. The American Near East Relief, sensing the same, began to transfer thousands of its orphans to Syria and Lebanon. That task was successfully carried out at Urfa by Dr. and Mrs. Jacob Kuenzler.

When Mrs. Kuenzler heard that my family, too, needed to go to Aleppo, she personally took them in her automobile from Urfa to Jarablous for the train to Aleppo. Mr. Hovsep Alahaydoian, her business manager and our personal friend, made the necessary physical arrangements. Among the items which Marie and her mother were able to take along with them were the papers Hripsime had buried in our backyard at the time of my arrest. These included the diary which has furnished some of the data for writing these memoirs.

On November 27, 1922, when my companions and I were entering the Criminal Court for the last time, a policeman handed me a telegram. It was from Marie and said, "We arrived safely in Aleppo." I cannot express how happy that telegram made me. Praise God! My family was free. At the same time, I was going to be free to attempt to escape, however dangerous that might be.

38. "The Snare Is Broken"

During the trial Ismael Bey once more questioned us thoroughly, and we gave our answers. He gave his verdict as follows: "Although these persons have committed no obvious crime against the government or the Fatherland, nevertheless since the photograph of the bones which they have depicted gives room for suspicion, I sentence them to eighteen months in prison." He asked the clerk, "Tell me, how many more months do they have to stay to complete their sentence?" The clerk reported, "Your Honor, they have already stayed three months longer than the required term." Said the judge, "In that case, they must be released from prison and returned to Urfa under guard, where they must remain under probation restricted within the city limits, to await the final decree from Mustafa Kemal Pasha."

The police took us back to the prison for official release. Soon afterwards the warden entered and confirmed our sentence, telling us that we were free to depart for Urfa. Truly a miracle! Until that day, of the hundreds of Armenians who had been sent to Diarbakir, we would be the first to return to Urfa alive. We were all paralyzed with joy for a few minutes. All the prisoners, especially the Kurds, congratulated us. Some said, "Hoja Effendi, we are very happy for your liberation, but we are going to feel an emptiness when you are gone." Wishing them all freedom, we went out of the prison hovel. The iron gates were opened, and we began to breathe and walk like free men, with the hope of remaining alive. "The snare was broken, and we were escaped" (Psalms 124:7). I reminded my friends of Ismael Bey's advice to leave Turkey at once.

We were ordered to be ready for Urfa the following morning. Until then, we were given free time. Immediately upon leaving the prison, Vasil Sabagh and I went to the Armenian Catholic Church of Diarbakir, which was open, and, kneeling, we prayed. After leaving the church, I sent a wire to Marie letting her know of our release from prison. (That telegram arrived in Aleppo one week after I did.) The next day we travelled by cart to Urfa accompanied by our police escort. Once inside Urfa, we were left alone. We were required only to report daily at government headquarters.

The Armenian section of the city was once more stripped of Armenian inhabitants. So I went directly to the home of one of my Assyrian parishioners, Mr. Monifar Alajaji. All my Assyrian congregation were

152

delighted to see me. They were amazed that I had been able to return alive.

Before leaving Urfa forever, I wanted to say a final good-bye to the Armenian quarter and to our magnificent Evangelical Church. When I entered the Armenian section, I saw everything deserted and in ruins. A frightening and funereal silence pervaded the area. It seemed the whole town was lamenting the loss of the people. This time there seemed to be a finality about the exodus. Engulfed in melancholy thoughts, I made my way to our Evangelical Church where I had officiated in the end; in which we had gathered the remnants of our people from the wilderness, especially our beloved children to whom we had begun to give Christian Armenian education; where I had baptized our first child, my dear little Alice. The doors of the church had been torn down. The narthex was dirty and deserted. On the top of the belfry was an owl lamenting. It was finally impossible for me to restrain my tears. Slowly I walked to the pulpit from which I had preached faith and hope. Alas, that hope had changed entirely to disappointment. And what disappointment! With tearful eyes I went out repeating, "My God, my God, why hast Thou forsaken us?" My only consolation was that a small segment of my congregation, among whom were my wife, my two children, and my mother-in-law, was safe and sound, free from the claws of the Turk, and I had hopes of joining them in a few days, only and exclusively by the grace of God.

39. Reunion

W ithout losing any time I had to get out of Turkey. My friend Mr. Monifar Alajaji found two Arabs who lived near the train station of Tel Abyad, just across the Syrian border from Urfa. We bargained with them: I would pay them five gold pieces (twenty-five dollars) if they would take me to the French commander who was at the Tel Abyad station. I had saved this sum from the money Marie had sent me. I told them, "If you take me safely, I will give you a recommendation certifying that you are dependable men; other Armenians will trust you and you will earn more money." They accepted.

Darkness fell, and the streets became deserted. All around the city were Turkish guards who arrested any who tried to leave the city without a pass. If it should happen to be an Armenian, they would beat him and put him in jail. We paid the guard on our route two *mejids* (two dollars), and he went away from his post while we were leaving, so that he would not see us go. The Arabs had brought me a fine Arabian horse. Brother Monifar told them, "This man has been in prison for twenty-one months. He is very weak. Wouldn't it be a good idea to strap him onto the horse?" They answered, "No, that's not necessary. All he has to do is to hang on tight to the horse's mane. He will be safe." The Arabs mounted their horses and I mine. We started out of the city, risking arrest and death. There was no other way to freedom and salvation. At three points on the way there were Turkish guards. Near the Tel Abyad station, especially, there were many gendarmes and soldiers guarding the area carefully.

After we had ridden several hours, my muscles became stiff; I had to dismount and walk part of the time. At the first two stations of Turkish guards we passed by at a distance without being suspected. But when we approached the border at Tel Abyad, Turkish guards noticed us avoiding the checkpoint, and shouting, *"Giavoor gechior, Vurun*! [An infidel is escaping. Shoot him!]," they started to run toward us. I had reached the final crisis between life and death. Raising my eyes toward Heaven, I prayed, "My God, if it is Thy will, perform one more miracle." The Arabs said, "Effendi, grasp your horse's mane tight, and pray. Don't be afraid." And they spurred the horses on. Thereupon our three horses sped as if with wings across the railroad tracks into Syria. I alighted and took a deep breath. Praise God! I was free from the gallows and from torture. It was hard to determine whether this was a dream or reality.

My Arab escorts warned the pursuing Turks, "Do not dare to pass onto this side of the tracks. This is Arab territory. You will be shot." The Turkish police complied: "We will not come there; just tell us which Armenian you brought over." Giving me one last measure of protection, the Arabs refused to tell. They took me immediately to the French commander's headquarters. Since he knew some English and I knew some French, he dismissed his Arab interpreter, then asked me for information about the conditions in the interior of Turkey, especially about Diarbakir and Urfa. He extended his hospitality to me that night, and the following day he let me join a contingent of French soldiers going to Aleppo.

When I arrived at Aleppo, it was dusk. I was impatient to reach my family. Since I was familiar with the Khendak-Jeddesi section of Aleppo, I went directly there and found myself in front of a coffee house, which I entered. Among the Armenians present, there were some from Urfa. When they saw me, they exclaimed in surprise, "He has white hair, but that looks like our Reverend Jernazian. No, it can't be — he and his friends were hanged." I said to them, "Fellows, it *is* I. By a miracle I have escaped." I told them that the five of us had been released. I eventually convinced them of my identity and begged them to take me to my family. Mr. Bamyayan, one of my parishioners, a former neighbor, embraced me saying, "O Badveli, what a miracle! Your family is staying with a Catholic priest near our home. Come, I will take you there."

It was a Sunday. Earlier in the day Marie had gone to the train station in Aleppo, hoping that there might be some newcomers from Urfa who might have news of me. Having seen none and heard no news, she had returned home hopeless and with tearful eyes. She was sitting at the supper table together with her mother and the children, but it was impossible to eat anything with such a broken heart. The two little ones, seeing their mother's tears, had been unable to open their mouths. It was at that moment that we reached the house and knocked on the door. The priest opened the door just slightly. Mr. Bamyayan said, "Father, please open the door; I have brought Mrs. Jernazian's husband, Reverend Jernazian." The priest replied, "No, no, Mrs. Jernazian's husband is in prison at Diarbakir; the Turks may even have hanged him by now." At that point, with Mr. Bamyayan translating, I began talking and tried to convince the priest that I *was* Reverend Jernazian, freed from prison by the grace of God. Marie heard my voice and said to her mother, "Mama, Badveli is here. Let's open the door." Thinking that her daughter might be losing her mind, her mother gave Marie a stern warning and a slap in the face. Meanwhile, from information I gave, the priest was satisfied that I was not an imposter, and let us in.

It is impossible to describe our joy. The priest and Mr. Bamyayan, deeply touched, left the room. Marie and Hripsime embraced me. My Alice and my previously unseen Samuel, now fifteen months old, clutched my legs. It was a day of rebirth and thanksgiving, and for this reason, since then we have celebrated my birthday on Thanksgiving Day.

When Marie had reached Aleppo from Urfa, she and the family had stayed at Uncle Astor's until the priest's apartment was found. Housing had been very scarce in Aleppo at that time, and only through God's special guidance was this place obtained. Marie and my uncle had looked steadily for two weeks under heavy rains. Then, one day, once again discouraged after a futile effort, they were about to return home when Marie noticed a house for rent. Uncle said, "Oh no, Marie dear, an elderly sister and brother live there; the man is a Roman Catholic priest. They rent out part of the house they live in, and no child has entered there for thirty years." Marie pleaded, "Uncle, let's just try once. Nothing is impossible." Finally, Uncle agreed to knock on the door. The priest admitted them and began asking for information: "Who are you? How many people will be living here?" When he learned that there would be two children, he said, "I'm sorry, but children cannot be allowed in our house." He explained that they had some rare plants in their garden, which children could destroy. Then Marie told him about my imprisonment and about her family circumstances, and begged him to let her at least bring the children for him and his sister to see. She assured him that they could be restrained. He was touched by her story and had a short consultation with his sister. They were sympathetic to my family's plight: "Very well, then, you may bring the children."

While Uncle Astor waited at the priest's home, Marie hurried off to bring the children. She dressed them in their best and brought them back. The priest and his sister took an instant liking to the children. He lifted Alice, and she grasped Samuel. It was as though they were welcoming their own grandchildren after a long separation: "The apartment is yours. Don't look anywhere else." Marie's young cousins from Mezire, Bagdasar Nanian and Giragos Gumuchian (whose father Nishan was the prominent dairyman tortured and killed in 1915), had survived in the desert and reached Aleppo. They helped the family move and get settled. The good priest and his sister had taken good care of my family. The children had been no problem. In fact, though happy at our reunion, the kindly couple were very sad to see the children leave when we departed from Aleppo.

Soon after my arrival, my three companions — Vasil Sabagh, Harutiun Dairmanjian, and Hagop Devejian — also reached Aleppo safely one by one. Unfortunately, Karekin Turyekian, the other member of our group, relying on protection by his Turkish friends, decided to remain in Urfa. It was impossible to persuade him to leave. Alas, only a few days after his arrival in Urfa, those very Turks he thought to be his friends had killed him in the street.

When Vasil learned that thousands of Armenian children were still among the Arabs in the deserts of Syria, he took it upon himself to rescue as many as he could. At that time the Danish missionary Karen Jeppe (who had served so well in Urfa) was engaged in rescuing Armenian women and children from the desert. Vasil joined her and threw himself wholeheartedly into this project, risking his own life. Vasil had been a confirmed bachelor before his imprisonment. After arriving in Aleppo, he visited us several times and told us that seeing our happy family life moved him to change his mind about marriage. After a short stay in Aleppo, he moved to Beirut, where he became engaged to a banker's daughter. He continued his rescue operations but set a limit. He planned to end his mission after rescuing the fortieth child, after which he would marry and settle down to form his own family. Why he had chosen that number, I do not know.

Shortly after my arrival in Aleppo, I received an invitation to serve as temporary pastor in an Armenian refugee camp at Beirut. Grateful for the opportunity to be of some help to my people once more, I left my family in Aleppo and served in Beirut for about six months. During this period I was able to spend every other Monday with my family. At this time Vasil continued to visit our home. When we left Aleppo, he was still actively working toward his goal. We were grieved to hear that he did not quite make it. In 1926, when he was bringing child number thirty-seven to Aleppo from the desert, the Arab from whom he had taken the child followed Vasil and killed him. To this day it is a painful thought that so soon after he escaped the gallows, he lost his life on a mission of mercy. Would that I could be near his grave at least to place a wreath or shed a tear!

Harutiun and Hagop remained in Aleppo. We ourselves had some critical decisions to make. Hopes for an independent Armenian homeland, raised by the Treaty of Sèvres in August, 1920, were dashed to pieces by the Treaty of Lausanne in July, 1923, climaxing a series of upheavals in the Near East during the three intervening years. Many of my friends urged me to go to America where I could be safe and free to lead a productive life, and where my children would have the best opportunity to become useful, Christian citizens. Also, I could not ignore my promise to Marie to go to her brother in America. None of my immediate family was left alive.

My Uncle Astor had returned to Marash in the summer of 1919, as had many others, with the hope of a bright future in his home town. Ten years earlier, in 1909, his son Shukru had left for America to join his maternal uncles in New York, and the younger boy Jack followed a year later. Uncle Astor, his wife, and three daughters had survived the massacre of Marash in 1920, had been able to escape to Aintab, then return to Aleppo in 1922. The two older daughters had shortly afterward joined their brothers in America. The parents and youngest daughter were now preparing to emigrate to New York, also.

One of those who encouraged us to go to America was Nishan Gagosian. He had been married before the war at his birthplace Pazmashen, near Harput. After the birth of his first child, he had gone to America. When the United States entered the war, he enlisted as a volunteer and fought at the front. After the armistice, hearing that exiles from Harput had been taken to Urfa, he had come there to seek his wife and child. Unfortunately, he learned that they had both died. During those sad times he found great comfort in visiting our home, and in time married a girl from our orphanage. We continued our close association. At the time I was arrested, his wife, who was pregnant, aborted and died. After that Nishan settled in Marseilles and started a hotel business. There he married a third time and had two sons. When he heard that we had been freed from prison and arrived safely at Aleppo, he wrote a letter of congratulations and urged us to go to America.

Miss Salmond, my orphanage mother, who had returned to Scotland but was still helping her former charges as much as possible, upon receiving news of my safe arrival at Aleppo, wrote to me:

> My Dear Ephraim,
> I was indeed most pleasantly surprised to get a letter from you, for I had thought of you as in the hands of those who might not regard your life, but Our Heavenly Father has some further use for you on Earth so your life is spared. . . . And now in Aleppo you meet many Armenians and I fear all in a sad, sad condition, but I hope and pray that God will enable you to be a Comforter to them even while you and they are under a cloud and there is so much that is mysterious. Still God rules, and "His eyes run to and fro throughout the whole earth to show himself strong on behalf of those *whose hearts* are *perfect towards him*". . . . Praying that God will *help* you, *guide* you and *show* you the way to take Ps. 25. 4, 5. . . .

Three months later Miss Salmond sent me forty pounds (two hundred dollars) saying, ". . . May you soon find all assistance so you can get away."

Actually, that gift completed our financial needs for the journey. We raised part of the money by selling some of Marie's jewelry and household goods we still owned. My past-due pastoral salary, held at the American Mission in Aleppo, provided an additional sum. I was able to recover it by presenting a validating voucher, one of the critical papers saved at the time of my arrest.

Obtaining our visas might have posed another problem. Some had been waiting three years. Ours came in three days. My colleague as interpreter in Urfa, Ibrahim Fawzil, was now working as a translator at the American consulate in Aleppo. He personally supervised the processing of our application and obtained quick action under a United States law which gave special precedence to clergy. We found out afterwards that we were the last family in Aleppo to be eligible under that ruling, as the law was changed to eliminate the special provision. God's hand most certainly continued to guide our steps.

40. New World

In August, 1923, Marie and I, Hripsime, and our two children arrived in America. Leaving behind our sadness at the loss of our native land, we were happy when we arrived at Ellis Island. With new hopes we looked toward the future. We were greeted at the port of New York by Hripsime's sister Mariam Garabedian, who had come from Providence, Rhode Island, to take us with her. But we were faced with a disturbing problem. The authorities refused to allow Hripsime to enter the country. They gave as reasons firstly, that the henna she had used on her hair was a sign of some disease, and secondly, that she was two hours past the deadline for entry under her quota. Aunt Mariam was unable to help, so went back home and returned promptly with her son Aram, a medical student, hoping he might be able to help keep Hripsime here. The authorities indicated that they would have accepted my mother-in-law if a male member of her immediate family could claim her. Only her son Hagop would have been eligible. But she was not permitted to wait in Ellis Island for his arrival from California, though we indicated he could be called immediately. Within three days she was shipped back to Marseilles, whence our ship had sailed. There she stayed for several weeks in Nishan Gagosian's hotel until Jack came east and she was able to join us again.

We stayed at Ellis Island about a week. Astor Shamlian's family had already arrived in New York and were living near their son Jack. As soon as we notified Jack of our arrival, he came to take us out. We had to declare that we had one thousand dollars, and Jack agreed to vouch for us financially. He took us to Uncle Astor's home where our belongings had been shipped. We were glad to be out of Ellis Island, where conditions were less than desirable: very crowded quarters, poor food, confused people, and stern and unsympathetic officials. After three days at my uncle's, Jack arranged for us and our belongings to be transported to Providence, where Aunt Mariam and her family helped us start life anew.

We had written Hagop immediately to come to Providence, explaining his mother's predicament. We wrote to Nishan in Marseilles to arrange for Hripsime to sail directly to the port of Providence. This time, she avoided Ellis Island and when she reached Providence, her son was there to claim her. We all lived together in a home near Aunt Mariam. After six months

Hagop decided to move to Boston. The five of us stayed in Providence for about two years.

A letter from Miss Salmond written on November 6, 1923, was most welcome during this period of transition:

> ... I am glad for every one of you people who have got to the US and would like to believe that you will not only be good and successful but will bring blessing to that great country. I cannot find any news of any Special Home having been found for the remnant of Armenia. Many efforts have been made. I have written to leading men and women of Australia and a great desire has been expressed but always obstacles are found and so far nothing is done. It is very mysterious indeed but God reigns and *rules* over all I am sure and if now we do not understand we can commit all to Him. . . .

I immediately accepted work in a jewelry factory. Marie did needlework. Within one year we saved enough to pay back our debt to Miss Salmond. We wanted to repay it as soon as possible so that our kind and generous friend might be able to help others like us. On May 1, 1924, Miss Salmond wrote:

> I do not know how you could earn all that money in such a short time, and now you must be careful and not undermine your health. . . . Last week a note arrived from Khacher Kalayjian who was a baker lately in Ebenezer. He hopes to get to the US but was asking help, so now I can do a little for him. He is now in Damascus. . . .

January 19 of that same year, Marie's 29th birthday, was a doubly happy occasion. For the first time since my arrest, I officiated at a wedding ceremony, that of my cousin Nouritsa Shamlian, Uncle Astor's oldest daughter, in New York. She married my friend Aram Magarian. Toward the end of the following year, the opportunity to resume my vocation fully opened up.

In 1925 I received a pastoral call from the Ararat Armenian Congregational Church of Salem Depot, New Hampshire. Beginning there and continuing in several other parishes on both the east and west coasts, we have been blessed with many opportunities in our adopted land. After Salem, we served in Troy, New York, and Boston, Massachusetts, and returned to Providence, this time as pastor, before moving to California. Here we served in Parlier and, in retirement, assisted as needed in the churches in Los Angeles. But the story of our life in the New World is a whole new subject and therefore not a part of this narrative.

God has given me the privilege of performing the marriage rites of both my children and the baptismal rites of my five grandchildren — Helen, Mari, and Theodore Haig, and Susan and Nancy Jerian (Jernazian). Marie and I continue to enjoy their loving presence. Alice's husband Vahe is the son of a fellow Tarsus College alumnus, Dr. Bahadrian B. Haig, who was also a teacher at Tarsus College. Later, Dr. Haig was a dentist in Beirut until 1922 and then continued practicing in Los Angeles. Here he again met Mrs. Carmelita Christie, the wife of our St. Paul's College president. She was the courageous lady who raised the American flag and saved so many Armenians during the massacre of 1909. She was now a widow, living in Pasadena. She and Dr. and Mrs. Haig remained good friends until her death. When we arrived in Los Angeles in 1953, Mrs. Christie had long since died. Dr. Haig's wife Helen was the sister of the "little mother" Azniv whom I had escorted from Tarsus to Marash in 1909. Helen died in 1938. Dr. Haig died in 1952. They had another son Robert who lives in Los Angeles. Our son Samuel's wife, Mary Aslanian, was introduced to us through Zarouhi Artinian, the sister-in-law of my brother Luther, who shielded me during the Massacre of 1895 when I was five years old. Strange and wonderful reunions all!

As I look back, I am grateful to God for giving me these years, and I cannot help but feel like a messenger of Job who survived through calamities and "escaped alone to tell" (Job I:19). I hear, also, the words of the book of Revelation (1:19): "Write the things which thou hast seen." And so I have written, as accurately as I can, about a small part of the story of the experiences of the Armenians in Asia Minor in the first quarter of the twentieth century.

My story is typical of many thousands. Revisionist historians and Philistines may try to deny or distort the truth for reasons of supposed political expediency or economic gain. But we who lived through those days know the truth and have faith in its ultimate durability. Innocent people can be killed by the sword, but the truth will not be killed by the sword. We have faith, too, in God's ultimate redemption of the Armenian nation, as He did for Job who remained faithful throughout his trials. After these innumerable tribulations, God will redeem and restore the faithful Armenian nation. "A bruised reed shall He not break, and smoking flax shall He not quench, till He send forth judgment unto victory" (Matthew 12:20). Justice shall prevail in the world.

Postscript

R ev. Ephraim Jernazian died on February 5, 1971, exactly fifty years to the day after his arrest and imprisonment on February 5, 1921. His deliverance from execution two years after the arrest gave him an even greater sense of mission — he was spared to serve his people with renewed vigor. In the New World, the needs were different but the commitment was the same as in the Old World. In the various parishes on the east and west coasts of the United States, together with Mrs. Jernazian, he helped the first generation of Armenian immigrants make the difficult adjustment to building a life in the new culture, and he taught the second and third generations to appreciate their heritage.

Reverend Jernazian was a true pastor in the fullest sense, meeting the spiritual and social needs not only of his own congregations but also of the Armenian community in general and of the American community. He had the gift of breaking barriers and building bridges, both among the elements of the Armenian community, and between the Armenian community and other Americans.

In 1953 Reverend and Mrs. Jernazian joined their children in Southern California. After his retirement from the ministry, Reverend Jernazian continued to serve others, through church and community activities. Also, expanding a favorite hobby, he established the Beacon Bookbindery, which became an outreach center in its own right: Clients came to receive not only their books bound meticulously and artfully, but also inspiration, information on a variety of subjects, and, when requested, helpful counsel. Even gardening, another hobby throughout his years in America, became a means of serving others, as the fruits, vegetables, and flowers from the Jernazian gardens were enjoyed by many friends and relatives.

Reverend Jernazian's funeral took place on February 9, 1971, the day of the great Sylmar earthquake. Although many were stranded and unable to attend, a full sanctuary of friends paid their respects. Reverend Jernazian blended spiritual and idealistic goals and standards with practical and realistic methods for applying those standards to daily living. His life was, as his name literally means, doubly blessed and fruitful.

Alice Jernazian Haig

THE ZORYAN INSTITUTE
SURVIVORS' MEMOIRS

Number 1. Bertha Nakshian Ketchian, *In the Shadow of the Fortress*. Cambridge, Mass., 1988.

Number 2. John Yervant, *Needle, Thread and Button*. Cambridge, Mass., 1988.

Number 3. Ramela Martin, *Out of Darkness*. Cambridge, Mass., 1989.

Number 4. Ephraim K. Jernazian, *Judgment Unto Truth*. Co-publication with Transaction Books, Cambridge and New Brunswick.

Number 5. Ephraim K. Jernazian, *Iravunke Jshmardutian (Judgment Unto Truth*, the Armenian text). Cambridge, Mass., (in press).

For additional information about this series and other Zoryan Institute publications, please write to: *Zoryan Institute, 19 Day St., Cambridge, Mass., 02140. U.S.A.*

The ZORYAN INSTITUTE is a non-profit, independent research center devoted to the study of contemporary Armenian issues in the context of regional and worldwide changes. It is wholly supported by contributions.

The Survivors' Memoirs is a series which introduces the experiences of Armenians who witnessed the Genocide and lived long enough to record their memories. It is a collection of documents reflecting first-hand accounts and impressions, beliefs and prejudices, fears, and hopes of individual survivors. The series constitutes part of the effort by the Zoryan Institute to gather and make available a variety of sources for the study of Armenian history and society in this century.